david olshine

STUDIES ON THE GO

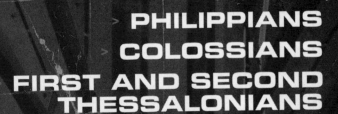

> **PHILIPPIANS**
> **COLOSSIANS**
> **FIRST AND SECOND THESSALONIANS**

ZONDERVAN®

outh
pecialties

YOUTH SPECIALTIES

Studies on the Go: The Letters of Philippians, Colossians, and 1 and 2 Thessalonians
Copyright 2009 by David Olshine

Youth Specialties resources, 300 S. Pierce St., El Cajon, CA 92020 are published by
Zondervan, 5300 Patterson Ave. SE, Grand Rapids, MI 49530.

ISBN 978-0-310-28549-6

Cover design by Toolbox Studios
Interior design by SharpSeven Design

Printed in the United States of America

09 10 11 12 13 14 • 20 19 18 17 16 15 14 13 12 11 10 9 8 7 6 5 4 3 2 1

DEDICATION

Dedicated to my wife and best friend Rhonda. You are a phenomenal support and a super mom who models the joy of being a follower of Jesus.

ACKNOWLEDGMENTS

To David and Leslie Crocker for allowing me the use of your getaway place at the beach. What a blessing!

Major thanks to my writing and research team, graduates of Columbia International University in Columbia, SC: Nick Cunningham, Mark King, Trevor Miller, Anne Lord Bailey, and Rachel Olshine—and to Rhonda Olshine, graduate of Asbury College and Asbury Seminary. This team has done a tremendous job of researching Scripture and writing with practicality and relevance for youth and young adults. Thanks for your diligent work and great insights. I couldn't have pulled this off without you!

CONTENTS

Section 3: The Letters of 1 & 2 Thessalonians

HOW TO USE *STUDIES ON THE GO*

Maybe you've tried to lead a study and ended up not knowing what to say or where to take the lesson. These sessions have all of the best ingredients for helping students and adults connect with God and each other as they encounter Scripture. These studies work best in a small group format but can also be utilized in Bible studies, Sunday school, youth group, or even road trips and retreats.

Before each of the three sections you'll find the Handy Tips and Insights: These three introductory sections help the leader or facilitator know some of the historical background and purpose of each letter.

Each session is then broken up into the following subsections:

1. **Leader's Insight:** A brief overview for each lesson to help the leader or facilitator understand the background and focus of the Bible text.

2. **Share** (warm-up questions): Before jumping in and studying the Bible, it helps to allow time for your group to connect relationally first. Warm-up questions are lighter and help your group get comfortable interacting with one another.

3. **Observe** (observation questions): These questions help your group—regardless of their Bible knowledge—focus on "What does the passage say?" and "What is the author communicating?" The goal is to bring to the surface what the students are noticing about the passage.

4. **Think** (interpretation questions): These are a set of questions helping your group consider what the author meant when he wrote the letters. The goal is to discover what the writer was saying to his audience.

5. **Apply** (application questions): These questions are focused on helping the group connect God's truth to their own lives.

6. Do: An additional activity option that helps students experientially "flesh out" the lesson. The goal here is action, putting head knowledge into real-life practice.

7. Quiet Time Reflections: One reproducible handout page for each session providing additional exercises to help students personally reflect on the passages on a daily basis.

My hope is that these studies create an environment where students and adults experience community, meaning everyone, being valued and respected. The leader's job is to facilitate a safe place in which people can be known and share freely. The best small groups are fluid, organized, free-flowing—with each person sharing. May God bless you as you engage students in the process of applying God's truth to their lives.

Blessings,

David Olshine

SECTION 1
THE LETTER TO THE PHILIPPIANS

HANDY TIPS AND INSIGHTS FOR PHILIPPIANS

WHO? This letter to the Philippians was written by Paul, a zealous Jewish leader, who had an encounter with Jesus that radically altered his life (Acts 7:51-60 and 9:1-31). His name was originally Saul and later became Paul (Acts 13:9). Besides Jesus Christ, few have shaped the course of history as the apostle Paul did. Paul was deeply rooted in the Jewish community when he encountered Jesus. One would think Paul's main calling after his conversion (or completion) to Jesus would be directed primarily to the audience he knew and loved the most, the Jewish people. And yet Jesus' call was for Paul to immerse himself primarily in the Gentile, non-Jewish community. He won many Jewish people to Jesus, but the focus of his ministry was primarily with non-Jewish people.

WHERE? Philippi was the first church Paul planted in Europe around AD 50-52. He planted the church on his second missionary journey (see Acts 16:12-15). Philippi was located 10 miles from Neapolis on the Aegean Sea. The main highway to the west, the Via Egnatia, passed through Philippi and made this Roman colony a strategic place to share about Jesus. The city was founded and named after Phillip, the father of Alexander the Great.

WHEN? Paul authored this letter around AD 61-64, about 10 years after he founded this congregation and about four years after his last visit from his missionary journeys.

WHAT? Luke, the physician and author of the gospel of Luke, was pastor of this church the first six years. Paul dictated this letter to Timothy, a native of Lystra (Acts 16:1) whose mother was Jewish and father Greek. The apostle Paul led Timothy to Jesus (1 Timothy 1:2), and Timothy joined Paul on journeys to Troas, Philippi, Berea, and Thessalonica.

Paul starts his letters with a greeting—"Grace and peace to you"—and usually a prayer of thanks and mentioning some people he cares about deeply. Philippians is a letter of appreciation to this group of Christians. Paul mentions the Philippians' partnership in the gospel (Philippians 1:5), which refers to their financial gift sent to Paul to help spread the good news.

Paul had a deep commitment and affection for the Philippian church. He referred to them as "brothers and sisters, you whom I love and long for, my joy and crown" (Philippians 4:1).

Written from prison, Paul's letter can be broken down into these chapter themes.

> Chapter 1—joy in suffering
>
> Chapter 2—joy in serving
>
> Chapter 3—joy in knowing Jesus
>
> Chapter 4—joy in contentment

SESSION 1
Joy in the Journey: Philippians 1:1-6

LEADER'S INSIGHT

Paul writes with Timothy as a servant and apostle (one who was sent forth) by God. We use the word *missionary* often in place of the word *apostle*. The apostle Paul went from being a persecutor of Christians to a preacher for Jesus, which landed him in the final years of his life as a prisoner for his newfound faith. Around AD 61-64 Paul wrote a letter from prison to encourage the Christians in a Roman colony called Philippi located in northern Greece (called Macedonia in Paul's day).

Paul took many journeys to spread the message of the Messiah Jesus (*Yeshua* in Hebrew). One of the churches he founded was in Philippi. Years later, as Paul faced death, he wrote these Christians to encourage them. His central point: We find joy in walking with God, joy in being a follower of Jesus, joy in talking and listening to God, and joy in working together to reach people for Jesus.

What's a Christian? Someone who invites Jesus into her life, then partners with God, resulting in good works in and through her. And the result is joy. More than 16 times Paul penned the words *joy* and *rejoice*. That was Paul's message in his time—and is still the message today. We find joy in the journey.

SHARE (WARM-UP QUESTIONS)

•If you could travel anywhere with all expenses paid, where would you go and why?

•What activity, hobby, or event gives you happiness or joy? Why?

•What's the difference between joy and happiness? Explain.

OBSERVE (OBSERVATION QUESTIONS)

•Read Philippians 1:1. How does Paul refer to himself and Timothy? Who was he writing this letter to?

•According to verse 2, what's Paul's opening greeting?

•Based on verses 3-4, with what attitude does Paul pray?

•In verses 5-6, what's Paul confident of for these followers of Jesus?

THINK (INTERPRETATION QUESTIONS)

•What's a servant? What does a servant do? How do you think Paul was a servant to others (especially churches)?

•Verse 2 refers to a saint. How would you define a saint?

•Look at verses 3-6. Why does Paul pray with thanksgiving and with joy?

•What's the promise to Christians in verse 6?

APPLY (APPLICATION QUESTIONS)

- How's your joy meter lately, based on the scale of 1 being low and 10 being high?

- Do you think joy is an emotion or an attitude? Explain.

- Why do you think many people have trouble being joyful?

- Where do you see God working in your life now? What work do you hope God will "carry to completion" in your life?

- What's one step you can take this week to choose joy in the journey?

DO (OPTIONAL ACTIVITY)

Have everyone in your group write down two or three stop signs or road blocks that keep them from experiencing joy in the journey. Then have everyone write down two or three green lights or triggers that help pave their way to joy. Then have each person share his answers with the group. Close in prayer, asking God to help the students walk in confidence that God's work is being completed in them.

QUIET TIME REFLECTIONS

Day one: Philippians 1:1

1. What word or phrase jumps out to you? Why?

2. Do you view yourself as a servant? Why or why not?

3. Think about the word *saint*. What does it mean for your life?

Day two: Philippians 1:2

1. What word or phrase jumps out to you? Why?

2. What does it mean to have grace and peace? What does it mean to have peace from God? What person in your life needs this grace and peace right now?

3. Think about God as father. How does viewing God as father affect you negatively or positively?

Day three: Philippians 1:3

1. What word or phrase jumps out to you? Why?

2. What do you think about the phrase "I thank my God"? Is it hard for you to be thankful? Why?

3. What are some ways to express thankfulness to God?

Day four: Philippians 1:4

1. What word or phrase jumps out to you? Why?

2. What's your prayer life like these days?

3. How do you handle what seem to be unanswered prayers? Why should we pray even when we don't feel anything? Think about

practical ways to develop a joyful prayer life (see Romans 1:10) and jot down a couple.

Day five: Philippians 1:5

1. What word or phrase jumps out to you? Why?

2. What does it mean to have a "partnership with someone in the gospel"?

3. Think about the powerful connection we can have with friends in sharing the good news of Jesus. What's one way you might share Jesus with someone this week?

Day six: Philippians 1:6

1. What word or phrase jumps out to you? Why?

2. What does it mean that God will complete the good work "until the day of Christ Jesus"?

3. In what ways does your life feel lacking? How might God intend for you to finish this journey strong even though you feel those places of weakness?

Day seven: Philippians 1:1-6

Read through the entire passage. Write down the one verse that impacted you the most this week. Commit the passage to memory.

SESSION 2
Facing Suffering: Philippians 1:7-13

LEADER'S INSIGHT

There was a banner over my gym locker room that declared, "No pain, no gain." Perhaps Paul would agree. I'm not sure I liked the reality this sign reminded me of each time I entered the locker room. Few people enjoy pain. I can't imagine someone getting out of bed, looking in the mirror, and praying, "God, please let me suffer today."

Job 1:1 says, "In this land of Uz there lived a man whose name was Job. This man was blameless and upright; he feared God and shunned evil." Yet cataclysmic suffering bombarded this man. He suffered by losing his land, livestock, his home, and then all 10 of his children. Talk about unspeakable grief! But Job responds, "Shall we accept good from God, and not trouble?" (Job 2:10a) I love the next part of the verse: "In all this, Job did not sin in what he said" (2:10b).

The apostle Paul insists walking with God isn't easy; in fact, it can be downright hard. Paul was writing from prison and "in chains" (Philippians 1:7). Why was Paul in prison? He was there because of his defense of the good news of Jesus.

What attitude did Job and Paul model while they suffered? We don't find them having a pity party, whining, complaining, or blaming much. Job worshiped God, and Paul thought of and prayed for the church of Philippi. In this session we'll learn how Paul prayed when facing suffering and how we can adopt that same attitude of prayer in tough times.

SHARE

•What would be the worst type of suffering for you?

•Do you think the phrase "No pain, no gain" is true or not? Why? Explain.

•How do you respond when faced with pain and difficulty?

OBSERVE

•Read Philippians 1:7. What's Paul saying to the Christians in Philippi?

•According to verse 8, what's Paul's affection for the church based on?

•Based on verses 9-10, what's Paul's prayer?

•In verses 9-11, what does Paul say the ultimate purpose in life is?

THINK

•Look at verse 7. Paul speaks of God's grace. How would you define grace?

•How is the "affection of Christ Jesus" different from any other kind of affection (see verse 8)?

•Verses 9-10 speak about our love abounding "more and more in knowledge and depth of insight." Why do we need love, knowledge, and insight? How do those help us live and respond to God?

•Verses 10-13 state Paul was thrown into prison for his faith, yet he seemed full of faith and joy. What do you think was his secret to live in the fullness of God while in chains?

APPLY

•What grade (A-F) would you give yourself on: a) giving grace to others? b) making good decisions? c) living right?

•Why do you think many people have trouble loving others? Who are some people you have trouble loving?

•If you could make the headlines in a magazine, newspaper, or TV for doing an amazing act of love, what would it be? Describe.

•In what areas of life do you need an extra amount of discernment and insight? Why?

DO

Have members of your group record over the next week every opportunity they have to do acts of love and grace to someone. Encourage them to chart out "win" and "loss" columns to acknowledge when they missed a chance or chose to ignore it and when they made a decision to do an act of kindness. Talk about their experiences next week.

QUIET TIME REFLECTIONS

Day one: Philippians 1:7

1. What word or phrase jumps out to you? Why?

2. What does it mean to defend the gospel (the good news about Jesus)? Do you share your faith with others? Is it hard or easy for you? What keeps you from sharing your faith?

3. If you were arrested for being a Christian, what evidence would there be to prove it? Identify some.

Day two: Philippians 1:8

1. What word or phrase jumps out to you? Why?

2. Whom do you pray for on a regular basis?

3. How might prayer help us love others more?

Day three: Philippians 1:9

1. What word or phrase jumps out to you? Why?

2. What persons can you pray for who need more knowledge and depth of insight? Do they need head knowledge or heart knowledge?

3. What does it mean to abound more in love of God and for people? How can you grow in this area?

Day four: Philippians 1:10

1. What word or phrase jumps out to you? Why?

2. What does it mean to be pure and blameless?

3. Think about the ways Jesus was pure and blameless in everyday life. How can you imitate his example?

Day five: Philippians 1:11

1. What word or phrase jumps out to you? Why?

2. What does it mean to be filled with the fruit of righteousness?

3. Think about how God calls us to be examples to others of Jesus' life. What might this be about in your life? List some ideas.

Day six: Philippians 1:12-13

1. What word or phrase jumps out to you? Why?

2. Why do you think Paul didn't get bitter over being treated unfairly and unjustly?

3. Think about how Paul made an impact to advance the good news. What are some ways your church and youth group can do the same?

Day seven: Philippians 1:7-13

Read through the entire passage. Write down the one verse that impacted you the most this week. Commit the passage to memory.

SESSION 3
Move the Chains: Philippians 1:14-30

LEADER'S INSIGHT

In football when the chains are moved, it means the offensive team made forward progress. (For those non-football fans, the goal is to score a touchdown.) In these verses Paul explains that what's happening to him is for a greater purpose. He was in prison, and he was getting the chance to express his faith to the palace guards. Often people complain about their situations and circumstances. Not Paul! The Romans used a rotation of guards on a regular basis, so Paul, in a given two-year period, possibly told thousands of guards the message of Jesus!

In this part of the letter Paul tells the church at Philippi he's torn by the present and future dilemma. On one hand, Paul was excited to stay on earth to represent and present Jesus. On the other side, Paul was getting ready to "depart and be with Christ, which is better by far; but it is more necessary for you that I remain in the body" (Philippians 1:23). Paul would die for his faith.

Paul was wrestling with wanting to impact people here and now, but also knew his time for death was coming soon. Paul states, "For to me, to live is Christ" and his mission was knowing God (Philippians 1:21). He was struggling because he knew he also wanted to be with Christ. Paul's motivation was for the followers of Jesus in Philippi: "for you" and for "your progress" (1:25).

The end of chapter 1 gives Paul's challenge to live a life on earth "worthy of the gospel of Christ" and his understanding that being a Jesus follower is a calling to "not only believe on him, but also to suffer for him" (1:27, 29). This session your students will see Paul's chains were being moved for the sake of others. God can use bad stuff and work it for good. Move the chains!

SHARE

- Have you ever seen someone preaching on the streets? What do you think about that method?

- Are there some TV preachers who turn you off? Why?

- Is it ever possible to speak about God without using words?

OBSERVE

- Read Philippians 1:14. How has Paul's imprisonment advanced the work of the kingdom?

- Based on verses 15-19, what are good and bad motivations for preaching about Jesus?

- Look at verses 20-26 and explain Paul's concern about the present and the future.

- In verses 27-30, what's Paul's view of living for Christ?

THINK

- Why do you think Paul tells us about his imprisonment in verses 12-14?

- What are some improper motives of sharing the gospel with people based on verses 15-19?

- Look at verses 20-26. Why was Paul struggling with staying on earth or going to heaven?

•What are some of the reasons people are afraid of suffering for Jesus?

APPLY

•Have you ever struggled with wanting to stay on earth or leave this planet to be with Jesus? What caused these feelings?

•Why do you think Christianity and suffering seem to go hand in hand?

•What does it look like for you to conduct yourself "worthy of the gospel"?

•If you died, what do you think people would say about you at your funeral?

DO

Take your group to a nursing home or assisted living facility. Spend time with some of the residents. Have students interview some residents if possible (or you could do this as leader), with some of these questions: Where were you born? Tell me about your family. Tell me about your faith. Do you fear aging? Share a favorite memory with us.

Afterwards process with your students how they felt about the experience. Ask questions like, **How did the person you met with feel about getting older? About dying? What fears did she have? What expectations did she have of heaven and the afterlife?**

QUIET TIME REFLECTIONS

Day one: Philippians 1:12-14

1. What word or phrase jumps out to you? Why?

2. How can suffering be used positively?

3. Think about how God uses suffering for his purposes. How might God use suffering in your life?

Day two: Philippians 1:15-17

1. What word or phrase jumps out to you? Why?

2. How can preaching the gospel with bad motives turn out for the good?

3. Think about the possible selfish and unselfish motives you have for being a Christian. What are some of these motives (reasons)?

Day three: Philippians 1:18-19

1. What word or phrase jumps out to you? Why?

2. Why do you think it's important for you to share about Jesus with others?

3. Think about some ways to preach Jesus without using words. List some ideas.

Day four: Philippians 1:20-22

1. What word or phrase jumps out to you? Why?

2. What do you think is the difference between Paul's desire to be with Jesus in heaven and suicidal thoughts? Is there any difference? Explain.

3. What are some reasons to stay on earth for a long life? What are some reasons you might want to die and be with Jesus?

Day five: Philippians 1:23-26

1. What word or phrase jumps out to you? Why?

2. Why is Paul so troubled in these verses? Have you ever longed to be with Jesus in heaven?

3. Paul tells us going to be with Christ is "better by far" than staying on earth. Do you think that way about heaven?

Day six: Philippians 1:27-30

1. What word or phrase jumps out to you? Why?

2. Why do you think we're to believe in Jesus and also suffer? (See Matthew 5:11-12.)

3. Think about some of the ways we don't live in a manner worthy of the gospel. How have you lived up to and not lived up to this standard?

Day seven: Philippians 1:12-30

Read through the entire passage. Write down the one verse that impacted you the most this week. Commit the passage to memory.

SESSION 4
Imitating Jesus: Philippians 2:1-11

LEADER'S INSIGHT

A popular adage tells us, "Imitation is the sincerest form of flattery." Paul would've agreed: *Imitate* means to agree with and adhere to particular behaviors and attitudes. One of the main attitudes we find most difficult to imitate is humility.

Here Paul urges the believers in Philippi—and all believers—to replicate the very nature of Jesus Christ. This means having concern for the well-being of others and thinking of others before ourselves. We also receive encouragement and joy from serving others and living a humble life as Jesus demonstrated.

In Philippians 2 Paul goes on to express in detail how Jesus is the best example of humility. Jesus had equality with God but didn't use it for his own power or fame. Jesus' concern was to glorify God his father and further God's kingdom. Paul mentions in this passage the same desire Jesus prayed for in John 17:21: "that all of them may be one, Father, just as you are in me and I am in you. May they also be in us so that the world may believe that you have sent me." Jesus and Paul both desire us to be unified and like-minded in our humility. Paul reminds us that living with the humility and dependence on God Jesus embodied is our goal—to live a life of imitating Jesus.

SHARE

- Which famous person can you impersonate the best?

- When you were a little kid, who was the one person you wanted to grow up to be like? Why?

- Name some professional athletes who have trouble playing as teammates and being unified. What gets in their way?

OBSERVE

- What's Paul asking the believers to do in Philippians 2:1-2?

- From verse 1 and verses 6-8, where does a desire to be like-minded and compassionate come from?

- According to verse 2, how can we make Paul's joy complete?

- Whose attitude should we be imitating (verse 5)?

THINK

- Throughout this letter Paul offered encouragement to the people of Philippi. Why do you think we need encouragement from others?

- According to verse 1, what unified Paul with the Philippians?

- From verse 3, what's a danger we should steer away from? How does avoiding this temptation increase unity in Jesus?

- Verses 6-11 tell us Jesus' obedience ended up giving glory to God. According to Paul in what ways did Jesus accomplish this (see John 1:14 and Hebrews 5:8)?

APPLY

- Why do we most often think of ourselves before thinking of others?

- Name one opportunity you saw today to care for someone's needs before your own. Did you take the opportunity? Why or why not?

- What's one area of your life you'd like to become more like Jesus?

- Who in your life could you serve this week to help bring about unity? Who do you have trouble serving?

DO

Have each person in the small group do one of these acts of imitating Jesus this week:

- Eat lunch with someone you don't know and whom few people talk to.

- Give a gift of money to bless someone less fortunate.

- Volunteer in the children's ministry at your church.

- Invite someone new to church or youth group.

- Generously tip a fast-food worker.

- Meet a need for a stranger and don't tell anyone you did it.

- Write a note to encourage someone whom you know is hurting.

QUIET TIME REFLECTIONS

Day one: Philippians 2:1-2

1. What word or phrase jumps out to you? Why?

2. What are ways you find encouragement from being united with Jesus?

3. Whom do you find it hard to get along with? How could you strive to be more like-minded and bring unity to that relationship?

Day two: Philippians 2:3-4

1. What word or phrase jumps out to you? Why?

2. Where do you see selfish ambition most frequently in our culture?

3. How do you most often show others you value them? What are some new ways to try?

Day three: Philippians 2:5

1. What word or phrase jumps out to you? Why?

2. What characteristic of Jesus would you most like to express in your relationships with others? How can you increase this characteristic in your life?

3. What was Jesus' attitude in the gospels as he spent time with people? (Look up Matthew 11:29 for one example.)

Day four: Philippians 2:6

1. What word or phrase jumps out to you? Why?

2. What do you think it means for Jesus to be the same nature as God? Where else does the Bible mention this idea?

3. What are some ways Jesus demonstrated his humility? (See John 13:1-17.)

Day five: Philippians 2:7-9

1. What word or phrase jumps out to you? Why?

2. What does it mean that Jesus made himself nothing? What does it mean to be a servant? Is this difficult for you to grasp personally?

3. When you hear the word *servant*, what images come to mind? When is the last time someone would have considered you a servant?

Day six: Philippians 2:8-11

1. What word or phrase jumps out to you? Why?

2. What do you think it means that Jesus was "exalted...to the highest place" and given the name above all names?

3. Consider the act of Jesus going to the cross. How would your life be different without that sacrifice?

Day seven: Philippians 2:1-11

Read through the entire passage. Write down the one verse that impacted you the most this week. Commit the passage to memory.

SESSION 5
Let It Shine! Philippians 2:12-18

LEADER'S INSIGHT

It's staggering how stars in a cloudless night sky can actually illuminate the ground as if someone had flipped on a giant night-light. But the Christians in Philippi lived in a "dark" society with many false gods and destructive lifestyles (sound familiar?).

In this passage Paul speaks as a proud parent, challenging his children to shine brightly in a dark world by living blamelessly. He tells them to "continue to work out your salvation with fear and trembling, for it is God who works in you to will and to act in order to fulfill his good purpose" (Philippians 2:12-13).

Paul suggests that when followers of Jesus actually live out their new lives through obedience, this sheds light on the darker ways of those living around them. Working out our salvation is living it out daily. Paul isn't teaching us to work for our salvation, rather that works will naturally flow out of us because of our salvation.

Paul's reference to being "poured out" (verse 17) is a reference to the word for *Eucharist*, a word we associate with communion and the body and blood of Jesus. In the book *Jesus Wants to Save Christians*, Rob Bell explains—

> On the cross, Jesus' body is broken and blood pours out for the healing of the world. The church is a living Eucharist, because followers of Christ are living Eucharists. A Christian is a living Eucharist, allowing her body to be broken and her blood to be poured out for the healing of the world. (Grand Rapids, MI: Zondervan, 2008, p. 149-150)

Paul also exhibited what it means to be poured out, giving of himself, and following the example of Jesus, his Messiah. As Jesus poured himself out for us, he set the ultimate example for us to give our lives to others.

Why would Paul share his intention to rejoice even as he wrote from prison? This kind of attitude shines forth so all people might see "your good deeds and glorify your Father in heaven" (Matthew 5:16). Paul challenges us all to "shine like stars in the sky" as we "hold firmly to the word of life" (Philippians 2:15-16). Jesus is the light of the world who calls us to shine light into places of darkness.

SHARE

- Name at least four uses for light.

- If you could fly into outer space, what planet would you like to visit and why?

- When was a time in your life when you went against the grain and did something positive outside the norm? What did others think?

OBSERVE

- What are two things Paul says in Philippians 2:12 that show his intimacy with the Philippians?

- According to Paul in verse 13, who makes good deeds possible? Why would this be important to note?

- According to verses 14-16 why should we "do everything without complaining or arguing" (NIV)?

- What's Paul's response to giving of himself so fully it was as if he was poured out? Why do you think he responds this way?

THINK

•What does it mean to "work out your salvation with fear and trembling" (verse 12)? Is this a reality in your life?

•What are things you see in your world around you that point to a warped and crooked generation?

•Why does Paul use the image of stars to represent the way the Christians in Philippi should live?

•Paul says in verse 17, "If I am being poured out like a drink offering...". What might he be referring to? Have you ever felt as if you were being poured out?

APPLY

•Where do you see God working in you according to his good purpose?

•How do you see yourself being a light in a "crooked and depraved generation" (verse 15 NIV)?

•What's a way you could pour yourself out to bless someone around you who hasn't come to trust Jesus yet? What difference could your action make?

DO

Have students, in groups or individually, construct a mobile using stars for each hanging article. Ask them to label the top stars on the mobile "God's purposes." Then say something like, **As you go down the length of the mobile, label the second-level stars "Fuel" and write Bible verses on each star that tell God's purposes. On the third and final level label each star "Glow." On these stars write ways you can live out the truth of the "fuels" hanging above every day.** When everyone is done, hang up the mobiles in the classroom or at home as reminders to live as stars throughout the week.

QUIET TIME REFLECTIONS

1. What word or phrase jumps out to you? Why?

2. How could you work out your salvation today?

3. What's your response to the words "fear and trembling"? What new understanding does this give you about fearing God? What impressions might you have to let go of?

Day two: Philippians 2:13

1. What word or phrase jumps out to you? Why?

2. How has God worked in you before? How is he working in you now?

3. How can you learn more about God's purposes today?

Day three: Philippians 2:14

1. What word or phrase jumps out to you?

2. With whom do you argue the most? Why?

3. Think about what it means to grumble. Why is it so dangerous?

Day four: Philippians 2:15

1. What word or phrase jumps out to you?

2. What would you most like God to cleanse from you and find you blameless of?

3. Do you believe Jesus has made it possible for you to be a child of God without fault? If so, how does that make you feel?

Day five: Philippians 2:16

1. What word or phrase jumps out to you?

2. What is the "word of life"? How is it important for us to shine like stars?

3. What would you like to be able to boast of on the day Jesus returns? What kind of life do you hope to have lived?

Day six: Philippians 2:17-18

1. What word or phrase jumps out to you?

2. How can Paul rejoice in being poured out?

3. Think about how you sacrificed and served others this past week. How does that make you feel?

Day seven: Philippians 2:12-18

Read through the entire passage. Write down the one verse that impacted you the most this week. Commit the passage to memory.

SESSION 6

Fueled by Friendships: Philippians 2:19-30

LEADER'S INSIGHT

In this section Paul emphasizes to the Philippians the importance of being connected in relationships. God told Adam, "It is not good for the man to be alone" (Genesis 2:18). Most people interpret this verse in a marriage context, but it's also a universal truth—we need each other! Later on Solomon wrote, "Two are better than one, because they have a good return for their labor; if they fall down, they can help each other up. But pity those who fall and have no one to help them up!" (Ecclesiastes 4:10)

The apostle Paul probably experienced significant loneliness during his time in prison. In this section of Scripture Paul speaks of his best friends, Timothy and Epaphroditus, and how they influenced his life: "I have no one else like him [Timothy], who will show genuine concern for your welfare" (Philippians 2:20). Epaphroditus is "my brother, co-worker and fellow soldier, who is also your messenger, whom you sent to take care of my needs. For he longs for all of you and is distressed because you heard he was ill" (2:25-26).

We were never called to live alone. Paul would've been miserable without these relationships. It's in our DNA. We're wired for friendships: "As iron sharpens iron, so one person sharpens another" (Proverbs 27:17).

In this session your students will explore how isolation can be dangerous. We mustn't be fooled into thinking that with email, Internet, text messaging, and cell phones, everyone is connected relationally. Many of your students struggle with loneliness and isolate themselves from each other. They long for close relationships but lack the skills and understanding to know how to connect. We need to help our students see the dangers of isolation and seek to be fueled by meaningful, healthy, and accountable friendships.

SHARE

• Who's one of your closest friends right now? Why are you close friends?

• How would you define friendship? How many real friends can someone have? How many friends can someone have based on your definition?

• What are some of the qualities you look for in a friend?

OBSERVE

• Based on Philippians 2:19-22, what were Paul's feelings about Timothy?

• Look at verses 23-26. What were some qualities of Epaphroditus?

• According to Philippians 2:27-28 why was Paul sending Epaphroditus?

• Why should the Philippians have welcomed Epaphroditus, according to Philippians 2:29-30?

THINK

• Why do you think Timothy was such a caring person (see verses 19-22)?

• Why do you think Paul says, "I have no one else like [Timothy]" (verse 20)?

• Why do you think Paul highlights certain people in this passage?

• Why would sending Epaphroditus cause less anxiety for Paul (verse 28)?

APPLY

• How could you be a better friend to others?

• How could your friendship help someone else's faith? In what ways could someone's friendship help your faith?

• How do friendship and faith connect for you?

• How can you take a genuine interest in someone's welfare today?

DO

Paul was an older mentor to Timothy. Discuss some strategies with your students on this topic: How can I find a Paul in my life? Who can your students develop Paul to Timothy (older to younger) relationships with? Set up a plan to pray for a six-week period, asking God to help each student find an older mentor and a younger friend to invest in. Make sure to explain to both the adults and students about meeting in appropriate places and making careful choices.

For resources and ideas on mentoring, go to www.youthspecialties.com.

QUIET TIME REFLECTIONS

Day one: Philippians 2:19-20

1. What word or phrase jumps out to you? Why?

2. What example does Timothy set for you?

3. Think about how you've become the person you are. What person has impacted you the most?

Day two: Philippians 2:21-22

1. What word or phrase jumps out to you? Why?

2. How did Timothy become so important to Paul and why?

3. Think about some ways to let someone older help you grow into what God wants you to be. List some ideas about finding a mentor.

Day three: Philippians 2:23-24

1. What word or phrase jumps out to you? Why?

2. Who's a younger person you could invest in and encourage?

3. What are some ways to be other-centered (focused on others before yourself)?

Day four: Philippians 2:25-26

1. What word or phrase jumps out to you? Why?

2. Why do you think we resist helping people with their needs?

3. How can you become a person who's genuinely interested in others?

Day five: Philippians 2:27-28

1. What word or phrase jumps out to you? Why?

2. How do you think Epaphroditus spared Paul from more sorrow?

3. What are some areas of your life that currently cause others grief?

Day six: Philippians 2:29-30

1. What word or phrase jumps out to you? Why?

2. Why do you think some people are risk takers and others more cautious?

3. Think about some people who need to be honored today. Take a risk. Find a way to honor them. Jot down some ideas.

Day seven: Philippians 2:19-30

Read through the entire passage. Write down the one verse that impacted you the most this week. Commit the passage to memory.

SESSION 7

Watch Out for the Dogs! Philippians 3:1-11

LEADER'S INSIGHT

The Rolling Stones sang, "You can't always get what you want...but you can try sometime!" ("You Can't Always Get What You Want," *Let It Bleed,* 1969) We always seem to want something more in life. Just watch a kid in the toy store begging for a new toy. We all do it. We tell ourselves if we just had **[BLANK]**, if we were just like this person, or if we were able to **[BLANK]**, then we'd be happy. This isn't how life works, though, is it?

In this passage Paul warned the Philippians to watch out for people who define worth by what they have or what they do. Paul confessed that if anyone has a reason to boast of accomplishments, it'd be him: "I myself have reasons...to put confidence in the flesh, I have more." (Philippians 3:4). Next Paul lists his reasons to boast: Being a pure Hebrew and not a convert (his circumcision on the eighth day was a big deal, but I probably wouldn't want to brag about it on a résumé), a Hebrew-speaking Jew (a Hebrew of Hebrews), his obedience to the law (a Pharisee), and his devotion to living out what he believed (persecution of the church).

But then Paul assured the Philippians that all of his accomplishments are like a steaming pile of rubbish compared to Jesus. Paul explained that righteousness isn't something we earn, but something given to us based on the actions of Jesus Christ and our faith in him. Our self-worth should be defined in Jesus, not in what we own or have done:

But whatever were gains to me I now consider loss for the sake of Christ. What is more, I consider everything a loss because of the surpassing worth of knowing Christ Jesus my Lord, for whose sake I have lost all things. I consider them garbage, that I may gain Christ and be found in him, not having a righteousness of my own that comes from the law, but that which is though faith in Christ—the righteousness that comes from God on the basis of faith. I want to know Christ, yes—to know the power of his resurrection and participation in his sufferings, becoming like him in his death." (Philippians 3:7-10)

According to Paul our purpose is simple: To know Christ, participate in his life, and help others to know him. Everything else falls incredible, short and only satisfies for a moment. Our worth, our value, our purpose can only be found in the person of Jesus Christ.

SHARE

- If you could be granted any three wishes, what would you wish for?

- Would you rather be a person of great wealth or great influence?

- How do people most often define themselves—by what they have, what they do, or who they are? How do you tend to define yourself?

OBSERVE

- According to Philippians 3:1 what are we supposed to do?

- Read verse 2. What kinds of people are we to watch out for?

- Paul lists his reasons for boasting in verses 4-6. What are they?

- According to verses 7-8 compared to Jesus, what are all of Paul's accomplishments?

THINK

- What would the kind of people described in verse 2 look like today?

- Why would the titles Paul mentions in verses 4-6 be reasons to boast?

- Why do you think Paul considered everything rubbish compared to knowing Jesus (see verses 7-10)?

- According to Paul, what's the final accomplishment of being found in Christ?

APPLY

- Where do you spend most of your time, energy, and money?

- How would other people describe you? How would you describe yourself?

- What would be the hardest thing in your life to give up for Jesus? Why?

- If Paul is right, and the greatest thing is to know Jesus and to be made like him, then how should this change the way you live right now?

DO

Have everyone write a brief description of himself/herself as though it were going to appear in an article on Wikipedia. Read them aloud together (anonymously might be best) and discuss your reactions to each one.

QUIET TIME REFLECTIONS

Day one: Philippians 3:1

1. What word or phrase jumps out to you? Why?

2. What do you think it means to "rejoice in the Lord"?

3. Do you rejoice in God? If so, how?

Day two: Philippians 3:2-3

1. What word or phrase jumps out to you? Why?

2. What kinds of people is Paul talking about?

3. What does it mean to put confidence in the flesh? How do you struggle with this?

Day three: Philippians 3:4-6

1. What word or phrase jumps out to you? Why?

2. What is "legalistic righteousness" (NIV)?

3. What are some things you boast about?

Day four: Philippians 3:7

1. What word or phrase jumps out to you? Why?

2. What is the "sake of Christ"?

3. What are some things you may need to give up for Jesus?

Day five: Philippians 3:8-9

1. What word or phrase jumps out to you? Why?

2. Do you consider it a great thing to know Jesus? Why?

3. What's the difference between a righteousness that comes from the law and a righteousness that comes through faith in Jesus?

Day six: Philippians 3:10-11

1. What word or phrase jumps out to you? Why?

2. What does it mean to share in the sufferings of Jesus?

3. Is this something you desire to happen in your life—sharing in Jesus' sufferings? Why or why not?

Day seven: Philippians 3:1-11

Read through the entire passage. Write down the one verse that impacted you the most this week. Commit the passage to memory.

SESSION 8
Winning the Prize: Philippians 3:12-21

LEADER'S INSIGHT

The idea of grace—receiving something we don't deserve—is such a hard thing for us to understand.

In this passage Paul shares that we're to live in the shadow of what Jesus has accomplished for us. Paul begins the passage by reassuring us he isn't perfect—but he lets go of what's behind him and strives to live up to what Jesus has already given him.

Then Paul encourages the Philippians to follow his example and avoid living as "enemies of the cross" (Philippians 3:18). These people were living for "right now"—for instant gratification. Paul reminds them to invest in eternal things because their citizenship was already in heaven.

Not only do we get caught up in instant gratification, but we are also good at getting stuck in our past. Our mistakes and downfalls can keep us from receiving from God because we don't think we deserve God's love. Salvation isn't something we've earned—it's something we've been given. Salvation is becoming like Jesus.

The word *salvation* literally means "wholeness." God's goal for us is completeness and wholeness. Our lives should be spent reflecting the incredible gift God has given us; that's what salvation is all about. Salvation isn't fire insurance from hell. The prize begins now, not later. We start the process of knowing God today.

Some think salvation is primarily about heaven; it isn't. It's about heaven invading our lives on planet Earth. "Thy kingdom come, thy will be done." Where? "On earth," as it's being played out in heaven. The prize is both present and future tense.

SHARE

- Have you ever been given something great even though you did nothing to deserve it? What was it?

- How did receiving the gift make you feel?

- Did the fact you didn't deserve the gift change the way you handled it?

OBSERVE

- According to Philippians 3:12 why did Paul press on?

- What does Paul say he forgets in verse 13?

- Verses 18-19 describe people who live as enemies of the cross. What do these verses say about how they live?

- According to verses 20 and 21, where is our citizenship and what are we waiting for?

THINK

- Why is it important to forget what's behind?

- What's the prize mentioned in verse 14? (Hint: Read also verses 20 and 21.)

- Read verses 18 and 19. Why's Paul shedding tears? What kinds of people does he describe in verse 19?

- From verse 16, what does it mean to "live up to what we have already attained"?

APPLY

•What fears keep us from allowing Jesus fully to lead our lives?

•Why do you think it's hard to live like Jesus?

•Does something in your past keep you from moving forward? How?

•Our salvation isn't based on who we are or what we've done, but on Jesus and what he did. How should this change the way we approach God and how we live our lives?

DO

End the session by saying something like, **Think back to who you were when you first connected to Jesus. List all the ways you've changed and then list all the ways you'd still like to change. Pray to God and thank him for what he's done and what he's going to do for you yet.**

QUIET TIME REFLECTIONS

Day one: Philippians 3:12

1. What word or phrase jumps out to you? Why?

2. What has Jesus Christ taken hold of for us?

3. Do you press on to take hold of this?

Day two: Philippians 3:13-14

1. What word or phrase jumps out to you? Why?

2. Is it hard for you to forget what's behind you? Why or why not?

3. What are the goal and the prize Paul is talking about here?

Day three: Philippians 3:15-16

1. What word or phrase jumps out to you? Why?

2. What's the view Paul is talking about in verse 15? Is this your view? Why or why not?

3. How is God changing your perspective on life?

Day four: Philippians 3:17

1. What word or phrase jumps out to you? Why?

2. What example did Paul set for us?

3. Whom do you look to as an example? Why? Who looks to you as an example? Why?

Day five: Philippians 3:18-19

1. What word or phrase jumps out to you? Why?

2. How do you feel when you think about those separated from God?

3. How can you make an effort to reach the people around you with the gospel?

Day six: Philippians 3:20-21

1. What phrase jumps out to you? Why?

2. What does it mean for you that your citizenship isn't here, but in heaven?

3. What does it mean to be transformed into the image of Jesus Christ? How are you being transformed in the image of Jesus?

Day seven: Philippians 3:12-21

Read through the entire passage. Write down the one verse that impacted you the most this week. Commit the passage to memory.

SESSION 9

Dynamic Living: Philippians 4:1-7

LEADER'S INSIGHT

Did you ever get in trouble at home for fighting with your brothers and sisters? To experience truly dynamic living, we must learn to get along with our brothers and sisters in God. In this section of his letter to the church at Philippi, Paul encourages the brothers and sisters in Philippi to do just that.

Paul begins by reminding everyone they should stand firm by knowing who Jesus empowers them to be. He continues by speaking to two women, Euodia and Syntche. These two women likely were experiencing a personality clash. Paul encourages them to get past personal differences and work toward unity for the sake of the gospel.

Paul continues by talking about rejoicing, gentleness, and prayer. Whether in the face of life's most exciting adventures or its most terrifying disasters, Paul says we can find room to celebrate. He then says we should be gentle to all and willing to set aside our own preferences to consider the preferences of others—and in this way, protect unity.

Finally, Paul encourages us to pray, thanking God for who God is, what he's done, and what he will do. This session will teach us about how to live dynamically.

SHARE

- What two celebrities do you believe could never get along with each other? What makes them so likely to disagree?

- What type of person is hardest for you to get along with? Why?

- Do you think God wants us always to agree with everyone? Why or why not?

OBSERVE

- Read Philippians 4:1. How does Paul describe his feelings toward his brothers and sisters in Philippi?

- According to verses 2 and 3, had the disagreeing women ever worked together? How do you know?

- In verses 4-6 Paul encourages believers to do three things. What are they?

- According to verse 7, what's the result when we present our requests to God?

THINK

- In verse 1 Paul says we should "stand firm." How does he think we should be standing firm? (Hint: Also check Philippians 3, especially verses 17-21.)

- How would you define gentleness? Whom does Paul say we should be gentle to? Why is this significant?

- Is it significant that Paul says "rejoice" two times? Why or why not?

- What's the difference between prayers of petition and prayers of thanksgiving?

APPLY

- Whom in your life do you need to make peace with? Which two or more people can you help bring reconciliation and unity to?

- Write down three things in your life you can "rejoice in the Lord" for. What can you do this week to express this rejoicing outwardly?

- Write down three people you struggle to show gentleness to. Write down the reasons it might be hard to be gentle with them. Pray and ask God to help you treat them differently.

- Make a list of some things that are stressing you out. Then write out a prayer to God asking for help.

DO

Ask each student to share one thing he's joyful about and why. Then rejoice together in your own creative way. A few examples might be singing together, eating cookies or ice cream, playing some games, tossing a Frisbee, etc. Next ask each student to share one thing she's anxious about. Go around the circle and have each student pray for the person to the right and to the left. Don't forget to petition and give thanks.

QUIET TIME REFLECTIONS

Day one: Philippians 4:1

1. What word or phrase jumps out to you? Why?

2. What does it mean to be someone's joy and crown? Is anyone your joy and crown? Are you anyone's joy and crown?

3. Are you standing firm? If so, how? If not, what's bringing you down?

Day two: Philippians 4:2-3

1. What word or phrase jumps out to you? Why?

2. Is anyone pleading with you to get along with someone else? What's your responsibility and role in the situation?

3. Do you think that you will go to heaven? If so, how do you know? (See 1 John 1:3-5, Romans 10:9-11, and Ephesians 2:8-9.)

Day three: Philippians 4:4

1. What word or phrase jumps out to you? Why?

2. On a scale of 1 being hardly ever to 10 being nonstop, how often do you rejoice?

3. Is it possible to rejoice in God always? Why or why not?

Day four: Philippians 4:5

1. What word or phrase jumps out to you? Why?

2. If you were put on trial for not being a gentle person, would you be convicted? What about you would prove your guilt or innocence?

(If you're having trouble answering this one, ask your friends and family for their thoughts.)

3. What does it mean that "the Lord is near"? (See also James 5:8.)

Day five: Philippians 4:6

1. What word or phrase jumps out to you? Why?

2. How do you "petition" God?

3. Think about when you hear the phrase "don't worry." What comes to mind for your life? (Then see Matthew 6:25-33.)

Day six: Philippians 4:7

1. What word or phrase jumps out to you? Why?

2. What does "transcends all understanding" mean?

2. What do you think the peace of God is? Have you ever experienced it? Explain. Read John 14:27 also.

Day seven: Philippians 4:1-7

Read through the entire passage. Write down the one verse that impacted you the most this week. Commit the passage to memory.

SESSION 10
The Secret of Contentment: Philippians 4:8-23

LEADER'S INSIGHT

Paul begins this section with the word *finally*, as if to say, "Okay, this is the home stretch." It's as if Paul is letting out a sigh of relief and resolution. He certainly doesn't fail in finishing strong. In these 16 verses Paul manages to explain what things we need to set our minds on, to express his gratitude for the generosity of the Philippian church, to encourage readers to find contentment in whatever their circumstances (made possible only by the strength that comes from Jesus), to remind us God meets our needs according to his riches, and finally, to sign off with an endearing farewell.

In closing this amazing letter, Paul focuses on contentment. What does it mean to be content? And how do we achieve it? Will it last for moments or forever? Paul knew how to be content when he was in need and when in plenty (Philippians 4:12). He learned the secret of contentment. And what is that secret? Verse 13 tells us. I'm not going to tell you—you'll have to read it out loud in your group. Then you'll discover the secret of contentment.

SHARE

•Today what did you spend most of your time thinking about?

•When you hear the word *contentment*, what do you picture in your mind?

•Have you ever experienced contentment? Please explain.

OBSERVE

•How many words are used to describe what we should set our minds on?

•In what circumstances did Paul find himself prior to writing this letter?

•Through this letter was Paul seeking money or gifts from the Philippians? How do you know?

•How does God meet all of our needs, according to Philippians 4:19?

THINK

•What should we do with what we've learned from Paul?

•According to Paul, what's the secret of being content in any and every situation?

•Was Paul's relationship with the church at Philippi a new one? How do you know?

•Read 2 Corinthians 5:14-17 and Ephesians 5:1-2. Compare and contrast the concept of fragrance (sometimes written as "aroma") as used in Philippians 4:18.

APPLY

•What have you spent the most time thinking about over the past week? How are these things the same or different from the things found in verse 8?

•Are there any people or organizations you freely and joyfully give yourself, your time, or your money to? If so, how's it going? If not, what's holding you back?

•In what areas of your life are you content? In what areas are you discontent?

DO

Have each person write down his favorite movie, magazine, TV show, or song (as of today). Together, evaluate these based on Philippians 4:8. Spend time praying together that God would help the truth in Philippians 4:8 to be the description of your thought life.

QUIET TIME REFLECTIONS

1. What word or phrase jumps out to you? Why?

2. Grab a dictionary and look up the words used to describe what type of things we should think about. Write out a definition for each.

3. What have you thought about lately that fits the descriptions you found? What doesn't fit?

Day two: Philippians 4:9

1. What word or phrase jumps out to you? Why?

2. What have you learned through these past few weeks of studying Philippians? How have you put that into practice?

3. How have you seen God's peace at work in your life lately?

Day three: Philippians 4:10

1. What word or phrase jumps out to you? Why?

2. Whom in your life do you care deeply about?

3. This week, what can you do to show them just how deeply you care?

Day four: Philippians 4:11-13

1. What word or phrase jumps out to you? Why?

2. Describe the most exciting time of your life. Now describe the most painful or challenging.

3. Looking back on those times, how would you describe yourself during those situations (anxious, content, nervous, happy, etc.)? Explain.

Day five: Philippians 4:14-20

1. What word or phrase jumps out to you? Why?

2. People around us have needs we can help meet. Who is facing troubles this week whom you can comfort and encourage?

3. Do you believe God can meet all of your needs? How does that change your life?

Day six: Philippians 4:21-23

1. What word or phrase jumps out to you? Why?

2. Overall, what's been your favorite part of the book of Philippians?

3. Write a note of encouragement to a friend or family member. End the note with Paul's farewell: "The grace of the Lord Jesus Christ be with your spirit" (verse 23). Or if you would like, rewrite this farewell in your own words.

Day seven: Philippians 4:8-23

Read through the entire passage. Write down the one verse that impacted you the most this week. Commit the passage to memory.

[From *Studies on the Go: The Letters of Philippians, Colossians, and 1 and 2 Thessalonians* by Dr. David Olshine. Permission to reproduce this page granted only for use in buyer's youth group. Copyright ©2009 by Youth Specialties.]

63 THE SECRET OF CONTENTMENT

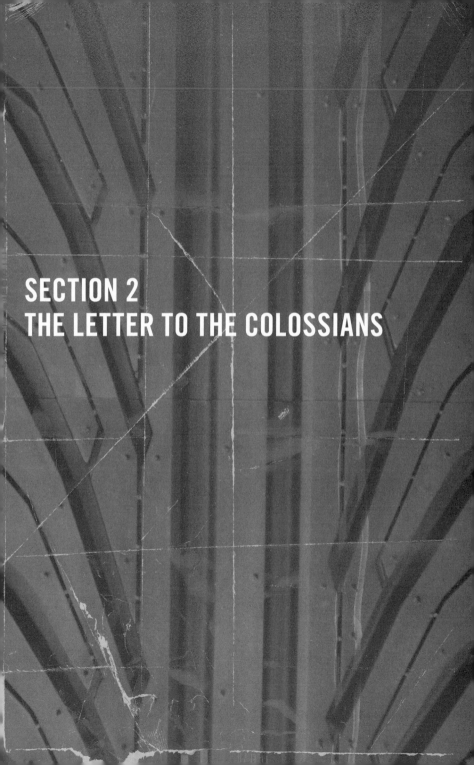

SECTION 2
THE LETTER TO THE COLOSSIANS

HANDY TIPS AND INSIGHTS FOR COLOSSIANS

WHO? This letter to the Colossians (pronounced *kuh-losh-unz*) was written by Paul around AD 61 from prison.

WHERE? The city of Colossae was about a hundred miles from Ephesus in the Lycus River valley. Located in the Roman province of Asia, which is Turkey today, Colossae was once a prominent city but by Paul's time had diminished as a prosperous city.

WHAT? Paul wrote to the Colossians with two reasons in mind: To encourage these Christians and to warn them of the false teachings infiltrating the church. Paul didn't start this church, rather Epaphras (Colossians 4:12-13) was the founder. The congregation was made up primarily of Gentiles who came to Jesus with a small gathering of Jewish believers. The church was wrestling with the heresy of the day: Was Jesus God or man? Or both? Neither? One or the other? Some teachers in Colossae were teaching that God can only be in the form of spirit and that the spiritual realm is good, but anything material (physical) is bad and evil. The problem with this way of thinking is, it leaves no explanation for Jesus, who was fully God and fully man. Paul addresses this issue in his letter, asserting that Jesus is both 100 percent God and 100 percent man.

This letter, like all of Paul's letters, addresses specific issues and beliefs the local community of believers was wrestling with at the time. Paul's letters were written to be read and processed by the collective body, not necessarily for specific individuals, although individuals could and should glean insight from the writings in today's world.

The letter could be broken down into these four P's:

Chapter 1—Praise of the gospel

Chapter 2—Purpose of the incarnation

Chapter 3—Practical instructions

Chapter 4—Power of community

SESSION 11
Have Some Fruit: Colossians 1:1-8

LEADER'S INSIGHT

The apostle Paul had never seen the believers in Colossae (2:1), yet he had a deep love and connection with them. As Paul wrote this letter from prison, he wrote with the authority of an apostle (meaning "sent one") by the will of God, sharing his excitement for how they were spreading the love of Jesus to others. Paul was thrilled by how their faith was enlarging day by day and how people were coming to faith because of their words and actions.

True faith is both vertical and horizontal. Paul emphasizes a deep devotion to communion with Jesus (vertical) and to relating with and loving people (horizontal). Paul mentions Timothy, and also Epaphras, who planted the church. Epaphras had visited Rome and told Paul about some of the troubling teachings in Colossae, which created a desire in Paul to correspond with the church.

The gospel is communicated as "God with skin on." God became human, called "the incarnation." As Christians, we can reflect the incarnation. Students can get a vision that their lives are making a difference whether they know it or not or sometimes even see it. Paul refers to this as "bearing fruit."

SHARE

•What are some of the ways you greet people?

•How do you let someone know when you're proud of him?

•How does it make you feel when someone encourages you?

OBSERVE

•Based on Colossians 1:1-3, what response did Paul have to the people's faith?

•Look at verses 4-5. What's Paul so excited about?

•From verse 6, what was happening with the gospel globally?

•What do we learn about Epaphras based on verse 8?

THINK

•Why do you think faith and love are mentioned together in verses 2-5?

•What do you think it means that hope (verse 5) is stored up in heaven?

•What do you think God's grace has to do with the message of Jesus (verse 6)?

•Why do you think Epaphras is mentioned in the first eight verses?

APPLY

•What are some ways to demonstrate faith?

•What things keep you from hoping?

•What are some ways to bear spiritual fruit?

•How can you be a more faithful minister for Jesus?

DO

Make a list, as a group, of people who've modeled faith and love to your group members. Have some note cards available and have each group member write a thank-you note to one of these people. (In this age in which handwritten notes have become a lost art, people tend to keep and treasure personal letters.)

QUIET TIME REFLECTIONS

Day one: Colossians 1:1-2

1. What word or phrase jumps out to you? Why?

2. Why do you think the writer mentions grace and peace?

3. List some ways to show grace and peace to others.

Day two: Colossians 1:3

1. What word or phrase jumps out to you? Why?

2. Why do you think Paul was so thankful to the Colossians?

3. Why is it hard to be thankful for what we have?

Day three: Colossians 1:4-5

1. What word or phrase jumps out to you? Why?

2. Why do you think Paul was so thrilled about the qualities of faith, hope, and love? (See also Ephesians 1:13-15.)

3. What are some ways to communicate faith and hope?

Day four: Colossians 1:6

1. What word or phrase jumps out to you? Why?

2. What does it mean for someone to bear fruit?

3. Why is it difficult to "truly understand" God's grace?

Day five: Colossians 1:7

1. What word or phrase jumps out to you? Why?

2. Why does Paul make such a big deal over Epaphras?

3. Think about some ways you can be like Epaphras to somebody. List some of your ideas.

Day six: Colossians 1:8

1. What word or phrase jumps out to you? Why?

2. Why do you think Paul talks about being faithful instead of being effective? What's the difference?

3. What does it mean to "love in the Spirit"?

Day seven: Colossians 1:1-8

Read through the entire passage. Write down the one verse that impacted you the most this week. Commit the passage to memory.

SESSION 12
Prayer Works: Colossians 1:9-14

LEADER'S INSIGHT

In this part of his letter to the Colossians, Paul pours out his heart with passion, beauty, and insight, asking God for some amazing gifts for the Colossians. It's apparent Paul had learned a most amazing lesson: Prayer works.

In this session your students will investigate one of Paul's most powerful prayers and see how this applies to our spiritual growth today. We will study not only the contents of his prayer, but also the basis of his authority in prayer—the power of Jesus Christ. Remember: Prayer works.

SHARE

- Were you taught a particular prayer as a child? What is it? When's the last time you prayed it?

- How would you rate your current prayer life on a scale of zero to 10, when zero equals "What's prayer?" and 10 equals "It's a part of my daily life"?

- Whom do you pray for most? What do you ask God for on her behalf?

OBSERVE

- Read Colossians 1:9. When did Paul start praying for these believers? How frequently did he pray for them? What's the first specific thing Paul prays for the Colossians in this letter? How does Paul describe the way God will answer this prayer?

- Read verses 10-11. Paul knows prayer works. He lists several anticipated effects in the life of the Colossian believers as a result of his prayer in verse 9. What's the first result Paul anticipates? What other anticipated effects are listed?

- Read verses 11-12. How does Paul describe the Colossian believers in these verses?

- Read verses 13-14. What do these verses tell you about Jesus? What has he done for us?

THINK

- Look again at Paul's prayer for the Colossians in verses 9-12. What do you think is the most important item for which he prayed? Why?

- What does this passage tell you about the Colossians' needs and about Paul's priorities and passions?

- What's the most exciting part of Jesus' mission to rescue us? Why? How is Jesus' mission connected with Paul's practice of prayer?

- Why do you think Paul spent time writing his prayer to the Colossians rather than merely praying for them? How do you think they might have felt when they read Paul's prayer?

APPLY

- What one insight from Paul's prayer seems most important to you? Why? What one element of his prayer are you in greatest need of?

- In what area of your life or future do you need "the knowledge of [God's] will" (verse 9)? What might hold you back from praying this kind of prayer?

- What area of your life needs strengthening so you can "live a life worthy of the Lord" (verse 10)? Have you seen evidence of God's strength or fruit in your life? How?

- Are you part of the "kingdom of light" (verse 12)? Have you experienced rescue from the "dominion of darkness" (verse 13)? How would you describe Jesus' search and rescue mission to a friend in need?

DO

Challenge your students by saying something like the following: **How do you want Paul's model prayer to affect your life? This week begin to take steps to learn how to pray Paul's prayer for your own actions and attitudes. Spend a few extra minutes a day asking God to do in your own life what Paul asked God to do for the Colossians. Read this passage in several different Bible versions, including Eugene Peterson's THE MESSAGE. Remember—prayer works!**

QUIET TIME REFLECTIONS

Day one: Colossians 1:9

1. What word or phrase jumps out to you? Why?

2. Why do you think Paul asks God to "fill [the Colossians] with the knowledge of God's will"? Why is this also important in your life?

3. Think about the areas of your life that need the direction of God's will. What are some? Ask God to help you know and do his will.

Day two: Colossians 1:10

1. What word or phrase jumps out to you? Why?

2. How do you think the Colossians must've felt once they read Paul's prayer for them?

3. What are some things God wants you to do or refrain from doing to live in a way that's pleasing to God?

Day three: Colossians 1:11

1. What word or phrase jumps out to you? Why?

2. What do you think was the Colossians' real need as mentioned in Paul's prayer in this verse? Why?

3. How does it make you feel to realize God not only expects you to know and do his will but also wants to give you power to do it? Spend time asking God for knowledge and power in areas of your life that are challenging or confusing.

Day four: Colossians 1:12

1. What word or phrase jumps out to you? Why?

2. According to these verses, what privilege is given to believers?

3. What does it mean for your life and future to have an inheritance in the family of God?

Day five: Colossians 1:13

1. What word or phrase jumps out to you? Why?

2. According to this verse, what two actions has Jesus taken on your behalf? What do you think this shows about Jesus' concern for you?

3. What has Jesus done for you—and how can we respond with thankfulness for this search and rescue?

Day six: Colossians 1:14

1. What word or phrase jumps out to you? Why?

2. Paul says God has provided two amazing benefits for us in Jesus. What are they? Have you experienced them in your life?

3. Take time today to thank God for what Jesus has done for you. If you've never done so, ask God for a part in his redemption and forgiveness.

Day seven: Colossians 1:9-14

Read through the entire passage. Write down the one verse that impacted you the most this week. Commit the passage to memory.

[From *Studies on the Go: The Letters of Philippians, Colossians, and 1 and 2 Thessalonians* by Dr. David Olshine. Permission to reproduce this page granted only for use in buyer's youth group. Copyright ©2009 by Youth Specialties.]

SESSION 13
What Jesus Has Done: Colossians 1:15-23

LEADER'S INSIGHT

People have many opinions today about Jesus. Is Jesus unique? Is he more than just a great teacher? If Jesus is God, what's the big deal? Some believe Jesus is just one of many ways to get to God. Everyone seems to have something to say about this man from Galilee. God wants us not only to know about him, but also to know him personally. The Greek word for *knowledge* means experiential knowledge; thus, when Paul tells us we need to know God, he is referring to knowing God through deep intimacy with God.

Having an accurate view of Jesus is of such importance that Paul spends a significant amount of time discussing it. The false teachings in Colossae were undermining the true nature of Jesus Christ. A group of thinkers called the Gnostics were spreading a false gospel of Jesus throughout the church.

The Gnostic teaching basically stated that the physical world is evil; therefore, God couldn't have created it. Matter is bad; spirit is good. If God is spirit, and matter is bad, then God couldn't touch matter. If Jesus were divine, then he could only be a spirit (not a human) in charge of the spiritual world.

Writing to the Colossians, Paul sets the record straight on the total supremacy of Jesus—reaffirming that Jesus is God (Philippians 2:6 and John 10:30-38 and 12:45), Creator, Lord, Head of the Church, reconciler, and redeemer; Jesus makes all things new and all powers and principalities are under his authority. This passage has so many important truths in just a few short verses. Let's see what Colossians 1:15-23 has to say about Jesus Christ.

SHARE

- If you could change anything about the way you look, what would it be?

- If God could have his picture taken, what do you think he would look like?

- Who do you think Jesus is?

OBSERVE

- Read Colossians 1:15-16. How does Paul describe Jesus here? What's Jesus' role in creation?

- Look at verses 17-18. According to these verses, why is Jesus so unique? What is his role with the church?

- Read verses 19-20. What amazing truths about Jesus are mentioned in these verses?

- Read verses 21-23. According to verse 22, what's the aim or goal of our reconciliation through Jesus Christ?

THINK

- Paul says Jesus is the visible image of the invisible God—like a photograph. In what ways does Jesus give us a glimpse of what God is really like?

- Verses 16-17 refer to the scope of creation through Jesus. What's the difference between saying "all things were created by him" and "for him"? What does this tell us about the origin and ownership of the world?

- Why do you think God made Jesus the head of the church? Of all the descriptions of Jesus and the church in verse 18, which one do you feel is the most interesting? Why?

•What was the purpose of Jesus Christ's coming to us (verse 20)? How did he accomplish the goal of reconciliation between God and people?

APPLY

•What priorities battle for supreme importance in your life?

•What areas of your life do you struggle to give God reign over? What holds you back from giving these areas over to God?

•Paul says in verse 20 that Jesus made "peace through his blood." Have you experienced this peace with God? Would you like to? How could your life change as a result of God's peace and rule in your life?

DO

Pass out paper to each member of the group and encourage each person to write her own list of 10 items describing who Jesus is and what he has done, based on what she's learned from Colossians. Then say, **During the week, spend time thanking God for his amazing gift of Jesus. Share your list with a friend, just as you would share a favorite photo of someone close to you.**

QUIET TIME REFLECTIONS

Day one: Colossians 1:15-16

1. What word or phrase jumps out to you? Why?

2. According to this passage, what do we learn about Jesus? What does "firstborn" over creation mean?

3. Think about Jesus as creator. What about creation is amazing to you? What creative gifts has Jesus put inside you?

Day two: Colossians 1:17

1. What word or phrase jumps out to you? Why?

2. What does Paul say about Jesus' role at the beginning?

3. Think about Jesus as the sustainer—that is, he holds all things together. What are some ways Jesus is sustaining you right now?

Day three: Colossians 1:18

1. What word or phrase jumps out to you? Why?

2. What does Paul say about Jesus in this verse? What does it mean for Jesus to have supremacy?

3. Think about Jesus existing before all time, at the beginning of creation with the Father and Spirit, then brought to earth as a human. What advantages in reaching people did Jesus have as a human versus when he was with God?

Day four: Colossians 1:19

1. What word or phrase jumps out to you? Why?

2. What does it mean for Jesus to "have all [God's] fullness dwell in him"?

3. Think about what it would be like if you were to open yourself to all Jesus has for you. How might your life take on new meaning, purpose, and power?

Day five: Colossians 1:20-21

1. What word or phrase jumps out to you? Why?

2. What's Paul telling us about Jesus' death on the cross and how that impacts our lives?

3. Think about how Jesus came to reconcile all things on earth and heaven. How can you be an agent of change for reconciliation on earth? How can you get reconnected with some people? How can you help the environment?

Day six: Colossians 1:22-23

1. What word or phrase jumps out to you? Why?

2. What do you think it means to be continuing on in the faith?

3. Think about friends and family who are not continuing on and take some time to pray for them. What can you ask God to do for them?

Day seven: Colossians 1:15-23

Read through the entire passage. Write down the one verse that impacted you the most this week. Commit the passage to memory.

SESSION 14
The Great Mystery: Colossians 1:24-29

LEADER'S INSIGHT

Some of the great books and movies of all time have an element of mystery. A good mystery keeps us engaged, sparking our senses as we try to figure out what's going on behind the story. This incredible passage in Colossians is full of mystery.

Paul starts by stating that part of the experience of being a follower of Jesus involves suffering. Jesus Christ suffered and we will suffer. Jesus says in John 16:33, "In this world you will have trouble." In Colossians 1:26 Paul describes a mystery that "has been kept hidden for ages and generations." What did King David and the prophets Elijah, Isaiah, and Jeremiah not know? What was hidden from them? Your students will get a glimpse of something remarkable in this session.

The Old Testament was based on the idea of the Spirit of God coming "upon" some person. The mystery Paul is speaking of is revolutionary and transforming—the Spirit now comes "into" people: "Christ in you, the hope of glory" (Colossians 1:27). God comes into our bodies through the Spirit of Jesus! Wow. God inside of us!

False teachers in Colossae were saying only a select group, a few chosen people, could experience spiritual completeness. Paul contends with this teaching by saying Jesus came to start a new community, and **all** could experience a new way to live. Jesus made it available to all! With Jesus living inside us, we experience the "glorious riches of this mystery": Christ in us (Colossians 1:27). The thought of God inhabiting our bodies through the Holy Spirit is amazing, not to mention a great mystery.

SHARE

•What's your favorite mystery movie of all time?

•Who's your all-time favorite hero?

•What are some of the best and worst mystery novels?

OBSERVE

•What does Paul say in Colossians 1:24-25 about suffering?

•What's the mystery, according to verses 26-27?

•What does "Christ in you" mean?

•What's the purpose of God for us, according to verses 28-29?

THINK

•What do you think the purpose of suffering is for Christians (see verses 24-25)?

•Why do you think the mystery mentioned in verse 26 was hidden for so long?

•What do you think it means that Christ in you is the hope of glory?

•How can a church help its members become fully mature in Christ?

APPLY

•Have you ever been able to identify with Jesus Christ's sufferings? Explain why or why not.

•What are some ways to explain to a skeptic that Jesus can come and live inside people?

•Do you sense Jesus living in you? How?

•What are some ways to become more mature in Jesus?

DO

Play a board game involving mystery, like Clue or even Monopoly. Then discuss what makes a mystery engaging. Ask the group some questions like—

•**Why do we like mysteries? Is there anything we dislike about them?**

•**When it comes to faith, do we want certainty instead of mystery? Why?**

•**Does God work more in mysterious or in certain, knowable ways?**

QUIET TIME REFLECTIONS

Day one: Colossians 1:24

1. What word or phrase jumps out to you? Why?

2. According to this passage, why does Paul suffer for Christ?

3. Think about some of the ways the church reflects Christ's suffering.

Day two: Colossians 1:25

1. What word or phrase jumps out to you? Why?

2. What does Paul say about the fullness of God?

3. What are some of the areas of your life that need God's fullness?

Day three: Colossians 1:26

1. What word or phrase jumps out to you? Why?

2. What does Paul say about mystery?

3. Think about the mystery of "Christ in us." How does this work?

Day four: Colossians 1:27

1. What word or phrase jumps out to you? Why?

2. Why is "Christ in us" such an amazing mystery?

3. Why can this mystery create hope in you?

Day five: Colossians 1:28

1. What word or phrase jumps out to you? Why?

2. Do you think of yourself as growing in wisdom and fully mature in Jesus? Why or why not?

3. Think about how our immaturity in Jesus influences and impacts others. What are some of the negative results?

Day six: Colossians 1:29

1. What word or phrase jumps out to you? Why?

2. What does Paul mean about contending with the power of Christ?

3. How can Jesus Christ's power change your life?

Day seven: Colossians 1:24-29

Read through the entire passage. Write down the one verse that impacted you the most this week. Commit the passage to memory.

SESSION 15
Marks of a Jesus Follower: Colossians 2:1-7

LEADER'S INSIGHT

The movie *A League of Their Own* (1992) is a story about a professional women's baseball league based on real events. In one scene one of the stars of the league, played by actress Geena Davis, decides to quit her team. She tells the manager, played by Tom Hanks, "It's just too hard." Hanks' character responds, "If it were easy, everybody would do it." Being a follower isn't easy. Sometimes following God is confusing and challenging.

Colossians 2 is a letter of both encouragement and challenge. Like a parent whose child is away for the summer, Paul reminds his church of what's most important—faithfulness to Jesus Christ. Paul is concerned that some in the church have been led astray by "fine-sounding arguments" or teachings that go against the truth about Jesus (verse 4).

Paul challenges the Colossians to be united in love and to continue to live and practice the teachings of Jesus. He encourages them to stand firm for Jesus and to continue to grow in him. "So then, just as you have received Christ Jesus as Lord, continue to live your lives in him, rooted and built up in him, strengthened in the faith as you were taught, and overflowing with thankfulness" (2:6-7). Let's look into this passage to discover the marks of being a follower of Jesus.

SHARE

- Whom do you respect and take advice from? Why?

- Do you think it's easy to be led astray from truth? Why or why not? What are some ways to keep from being led astray or deceived?

- Have you ever been deceived by someone? How did it feel when the truth came out?

OBSERVE

- Read Colossians 1:1-2. Why was Paul struggling for the Colossians?

- What was Paul concerned about in verse 4?

- What does Paul ask the church to do in verse 6? What does this have to do with Paul's concerns?

THINK

- Read verse 1. Why do you think Paul chose to start the chapter this way? What might've been the struggle Paul was facing?

- Why do you think Paul is so concerned with the church being united and loving each other (verses 2-3)? How would unity help prevent people from being deceived by false teaching?

- What do you think it means to have a "firm...faith in Christ" (verse 5)?

- What do you think Paul is saying in verses 6 and 7? What do you think this has to do with people being deceived?

APPLY

• What are some things that lead Christians to false beliefs? How could we help prevent that?

• How can spiritual leaders and other believers help keep us from going astray?

• Do you think you know the teachings of Jesus well enough to quickly identify when someone is teaching them falsely?

DO

Suggest to your group that they examine Bible teaching carefully by trying this exercise. Say something like, **This Sunday take a Bible to church or youth group and read along with the pastor or leader. Examine what the leader is teaching in the Bible. Not only will this help you overcome boredom, but it's also a great way to stay on track and not be led astray.**

QUIET TIME REFLECTIONS

Day one: Colossians 2:1-2

1. What word or phrase jumps out to you? Why?

2. Why do you think Paul lets the Colossians know he's struggling? What do you think Paul's purpose is (verse 2)?

3. Spend some time today thinking about times you've felt encouraged and united with others. How do you think you feel more stable and at ease in these moments?

Day two: Colossians 2:3

1. What word or phrase jumps out to you? Why?

2. Verse 3 refers to what is said in verse 2. In whom are these treasures hidden, and what are these treasures, according to verse 3?

3. Spend some time today thinking about the treasures of wisdom and knowledge in Jesus Christ. Make a list of some knowledge we as Christians have been given.

Day three: Colossians 2:3-4

1. What word or phrase jumps out to you? Why?

2. How do you think the treasure from verse 3 would help people not to be deceived? What knowledge or wisdom could help?

3. Spend some time today thinking about your faith in Jesus. Do you think you're capable of being led astray? How do you know if you have been?

Day four: Colossians 2:5

1. What word or phrase jumps out to you? Why?

2. Do you have people in your life who care about your spiritual life? What do you think Paul means by being present in spirit? How is this possible?

3. Spend some time today thinking about who guides your spiritual steps. Is it a man like Paul who teaches about the truth of Jesus? Does anyone guide you? Also, think about your faith in Jesus. Does your faith in Jesus motivate you to listen to others?

Day five: Colossians 2:6

1. What word or phrase jumps out to you? Why?

2. Have you received Jesus as Lord? Is he the king of your life? If you have, do you sometimes find it difficult to stay committed to Jesus?

3. Spend some time today thinking about your spiritual life. Jesus calls us to be different from the system of the world. We're told to be light to the world. Are you a light to the world? How?

Day six: Colossians 2:6-7

1. What word or phrase jumps out to you? Why?

2. Do you think this passage helps show the church how not to be deceived? How? Why do you think Paul writes about thankfulness? Do you think a thankful heart focused on Jesus might help prevent against deceit? Why or why not?

3. Are you thankful for the mentors and teachers and pastors in your life? Do they help save you from being led astray? How?

Day seven: Colossians 2:1-7

Read through the entire passage. Write down the one verse that impacted you the most this week. Commit the passage to memory.

SESSION 16
Continue to Live: Colossians 2:8-15

LEADER'S INSIGHT

It seems as if so many messages in our culture go against the teachings of the Bible. The messages of our culture lure us in because they don't initially appear to be destructive. This same issue was happening with the church of Colossae. Paul wrote his letter to try to help rescue the people in that church who were being led astray.

In this passage Paul reminds us that just as Jesus Christ died and rose again, we who trust in Jesus have been changed and made into new creations through the very same power. The phrase "new creations" in the Greek language communicates the idea of being morphed from one species of being to another, as a caterpillar becomes a butterfly. After surrendering our lives to Jesus, we become new species, so Paul is saying in essence, "Live like it!"

Paul tells the Colossians—and us—Jesus has changed them and wants them to live according to his teachings. Further, even though philosophy has some value, any ideas based only on human reason and experience are shallow and faulty. Paul explains that we need to interpret life with a godly, divine perspective and worldview.

When we accept Jesus' death and resurrection for ourselves, we undergo much more than a legal transaction from "lost" to "saved." Rather, we're then alive for the first time. Once we come alive, we must continue to live!

SHARE

•How do you handle teachings or ideas that contradict each other?

•Do you think the world's teachings and God's law are sometimes at odds? Why?

•Do you think Jesus always taught truth? Why or why not?

OBSERVE

•Read Colossians 2:8. What things were leading the Colossians astray?

•Who has the highest authority, according to Paul in verse 10? Why?

•How did Jesus fix what was wrong with us (our sinful nature)?

•In verse 8 Paul speaks of people being led astray by human reason. What do you think Paul means by "spiritual forces of this world"?

THINK

•Circumcision was a physical sign Jews performed to show they belonged to the family of Abraham, whom God found favor with and blessed. What do you think Paul means when he talks about Jesus giving a spiritual circumcision?

•Through Jesus' death on the cross, what powers and authorities do think he disarmed (see verses 13-15)?

•What sort of empty philosophies have you seen lead people away from Jesus?

•Why do you think we can trust Jesus?

APPLY

•Do you think Jesus has authority in your life? Why or why not?

•Do you trust the Bible's ideas over other conflicting thoughts? How might this be difficult to do sometimes?

•If someone says something that goes against what the Bible teaches, can it still be true? Why or why not?

•Why is it harder for some to submit to Jesus than others?

DO

Read back through Colossians 2:8-15 together, having students keep in mind what Jesus has done. Discuss with your group: **Is it enough for you just to believe in Jesus?** Then encourage students to spend some time this week thinking through some of the areas in their lives in which they may've been led astray from the authority of Jesus. Close in prayer, asking God to show students these areas in their own lives and to bring them back to God's authority where needed.

QUIET TIME REFLECTIONS

Day one: Colossians 2:8

1. What word or phrase jumps out to you? Why?

2. What are some human philosophies and thoughts that go against Jesus' teachings?

3. Spend some time today thinking about your beliefs. Are they at odds with Jesus and his teachings? If so, how?

Day two: Colossians 2:9

1. What word or phrase jumps out to you? Why?

2. What do you think Paul means when he says, "In Christ all the fullness of the Deity lives in bodily form"? What does that mean about Jesus' authority?

3. Spend some time today thinking about the completeness of Jesus. Do you think anyone else can speak for both humans and God?

Day three: Colossians 2:10

1. What word or phrase jumps out to you? Why?

2. Paul says, "In Christ you have been brought to fullness." What do you think Paul means by this?

3. Spend some time today thinking about the ways in which you're made complete in Jesus Christ. How should this affect what you say, do, and believe?

Day four: Colossians 2:11-12

1. What word or phrase jumps out to you? Why?

2. Paul mentions circumcision, a custom of the Jewish nation, to show a physical sign that they belonged to God. What do you think Paul means by a spiritual circumcision?

3. Spend some time today thinking about the power of God that raised Jesus from the dead. Do you believe in that power? Do you believe your sin was removed with the same power?

Day five: Colossians 2:13-14

1. What word or phrase jumps out to you? Why?

2. What do you think it means that our sinful natures have been nailed to the cross?

3. Spend some time today thanking God. If you trust in who Jesus is, then your sins are forgiven! Thank God for all he's done to cancel out your sin.

Day six: Colossians 2:15

1. What word or phrase jumps out to you? Why?

2. What has God done through Christ's death and resurrection?

3. Spend some time today thinking about the authority of Jesus. How might his humanity and divinity help give him authority? How did his death and resurrection give him authority?

Day seven: Colossians 2:8-15

Read through the entire passage. Write down the one verse that impacted you the most this week. Commit the passage to memory.

SESSION 17
Freedom from Legalism: Colossians 2:16-23

LEADER'S INSIGHT

A popular John Mayer song claims there's "no such thing as the real world" ("No Such Thing," *Room for Squares*, 2001). For a Christian the real world isn't materialism or the things of this culture. The real world is found in following Jesus. Unfortunately, the followers of Jesus who lived in the town of Colossae began to believe Jesus was the same as other gods and spirits. They also got overly focused on appearing like Christians rather than truly being followers of Jesus.

The Colossians settled for rules over a relationship with Jesus. When Paul heard about this dilemma, he wrote to his friends and fellow believers, urging them to place Jesus at the center of their worship, lifestyle, and beliefs.

When we choose rules over the relationship, the Bible refers to this as slavery. Jesus came to set the prisoner free (Luke 4:18). "Where the Spirit of the Lord is, there is freedom" (2 Corinthians 3:17). Galatians 5:1 says, "It is for freedom that Christ has set us free. Stand firm, then, and do not let yourselves be burdened again by the yoke of slavery."

A "yoke" in the Colossians' day referred not only to the wooden harness that fits over the shoulders of the oxen, but also to the burdensome teachings of some of the Jewish teachers who were caught up in legalism. Matthew 23 lists a number of Jesus' rebukes to those teachers, commonly called the "seven woes to the Pharisees."

Some of these teachings were so rigid, they became nearly impossible to keep. Paul said in Galatians 5:13, "You, my brothers and sisters, were called to be free. But do not use your freedom to indulge the sinful nature; rather, serve one another humbly in love." Freedom is empowerment truly to love and be loved. It's not about keeping man-made rules—it's about finding freedom through following Jesus.

SHARE

- Describe a time when you broke a rule and got away with it. How did you feel afterward? How do you feel about it now?

- Why do we need rules in our lives? What would happen if we didn't live by any rules?

- Do you ever feel restricted by rules set for you? Which rules are the hardest for you to follow?

OBSERVE

- Read Colossians 2:16-18. What does Paul say not to put up with?

- Based on verses 20-21, what does Paul say about rules?

- Look at verses 22-23. How does Paul feel about man-made rules?

THINK

- Look at verse 16. How were people being judged in this verse? Why do we judge others? Do you find yourself judging others? Why?

- Verses 17-19 mention people who are out of touch with God. How do you feel and act when you're out of touch with God?

- In verse 20 Paul asks why we'd let humans determine our actions instead of God. How do you fall into this trap? How can you break the cycle?

•Define the words *humble* and *show-off*. Do you think you fall into either category?

APPLY

•Why is it so easy to be judgmental? What makes us critical of others?

•Have you ever been on the receiving end of criticism from a judgmental person? How does it make you feel?

•Why is it sometimes easier to do what our friends say rather than doing what God tells us through the Bible?

•What's one step you could take this week to be more accepting of God's rules?

DO

Have each person in the group write down on paper two to three things he sometimes judges people about (outer look, clothing, attitudes, etc). Share answers with the group. Then have everyone write down two to three ways they can work on accepting people more and following God's rules. Then have everyone staple those answers over the first ones to signify a new start and God's direction in their lives.

QUIET TIME REFLECTIONS

Day one: Colossians 2:16

1. What word or phrase jumps out to you? Why?

2. Why do we sometimes put pressure on others to accept our opinions?

3. Spend time today thinking about how you sometimes judge others. How can you let God help change your heart?

Day two: Colossians 2:17

1. What word or phrase jumps out to you? Why?

2. Paul talks about diet and worship being only symbolic. Why do you think people in that time put so much pressure and influence on those things?

3. What does God value? Compare this to what you value.

Day three: Colossians 2:18

1. What word or phrase jumps out to you? Why?

2. How do we know which authorities in our life we should listen to?

3. Spend time today thinking about how you can help spiritually encourage your friends, rather than judging them. How can you let people spiritually encourage you?

Day four: Colossians 2:19

1. What word or phrase jumps out to you? Why?

2. What does Paul compare people who've lost their connection with Jesus to? What are some ways you can stay connected to Jesus, "the head"?

3. Spend some time thinking about how you've changed because of your connectedness to Jesus. How has that affected others?

Day five: Colossians 2:20-21

1. What word or phrase jumps out to you? Why?

2. What are some of the "rules" of Christianity you struggle with? Are these rules from the Bible or rules created by humans?

3. Spend some time today thinking about the spiritual freedom you have been given. What does it mean to you?

Day six: Colossians 2:22-23

1. What word or phrase jumps out to you? Why?

2. What does Paul say that man-made rules look like?

3. How do people sometimes try to show off spiritually?

Day seven: Colossians 2:16-23

Read through the entire passage. Write down the one verse that impacted you the most this week. Commit the passage to memory.

SESSION 18
What to Wear: Colossians 3:1-15

LEADER'S INSIGHT

There's nothing like a new car. You know it's new just by its scent. The people of Colossae were wearing a new scent, in a way. They'd become Christians but still were having a hard time turning from their old ways. Do you ever have a hard time putting your beliefs into action? As Christians it's sometimes hard to change old habits, isn't it?

In this passage Paul is writing to Christians to help encourage us in our faith and actions. Paul tells us life as Christians is completely different from how our lives used to be. We make a choice, empowered by Jesus, to be different and to act different.

We've been crucified with Jesus Christ (Colossians 3:3-5); our old nature of sin is dead (3:9), and Jesus' resurrection tells us that we've been "raised with Christ" (3:1). The whole idea is that when we stop living for ourselves and start wearing new clothes, we start being like Jesus and less like people who follow the system of the world.

We take off the old "smell" of our sinful lives and put on the new scent of Jesus. In John 17:15 Jesus prayed for God not to take us "out of the world but that you protect them from the evil one." God doesn't want the Christian community to be isolated from the world. We're called to influence culture (Matthew 5:13-16).

However, because of the power and pressure of Satan and the lures of sin, God does want to protect us. Paul urges the Colossians to allow the "peace of Christ" to rule their lives (3:15). This word *rule* comes from the Greek word *umpire*. In athletic games in Paul's day and in ours, the umpire (or referee) has the final say. Paul is saying to let Jesus' peace be the deciding factor in all you say and do—and put on the clothes of gentleness, compassion, and patience. What do you plan to wear today?

SHARE

- How does it feel when you buy something brand-new? Are you proud to show it off?

- In what ways do you see a difference in your life since becoming a Christian?

- Has being a Christian been an easy choice? In what ways do you still struggle with your old ways of living?

OBSERVE

- Read Colossians 3:1-2 and look at what Paul says about our perspective. How are we supposed to look at life?

- In verses 3-4 what does Paul say about your old life versus your new one?

- List the things we're commanded to get rid of in verses 5-11.

- List the things we're commanded to do in verses 12-15.

THINK

- What does pursuing the things of God look like to you?

- Based on verse 4, what do you think it means to make Christ your life?

- Look at verses 5-9. What's the result of our disobedience?

•In verses 10-14, what are the rewards of a new life in Jesus? What differences are there?

APPLY

•If someone took a look at your life before and after you became a Christian, could she tell the difference?

•Why do you think many people have a hard time fully embracing their new life?

•What are some things from your old life you still need to take off?

•What's one step you can take to add love to your "wardrobe"?

DO

At the beginning of the group's time together, bring out a plain white T-shirt and have each student write one to two sins or habits he still struggles with on the shirt. Then put the T-shirt in liquid bleach. Show it at the end of the group's time, then break the group up into partners and have partners pray for one another about those struggles.

QUIET TIME REFLECTIONS

Day one: Colossians 3:1-2

1. What word or phrase jumps out to you? Why?

2. How do you think you can see life through God's perspective rather than your own?

3. Take some time today to think about how you move through life. What will it take for you to be more alert to God's work and presence?

Day two: Colossians 3:3-5

1. What word or phrase jumps out to you? Why?

2. What are some actions you can take to remove things from your old life? Do you think it's possible to get rid of all of them?

3. Take some time today and focus on who the real you is. How do you want people to see you?

Day three: Colossians 3:6-7

1. What word or phrase jumps out to you? Why?

2. Is your life shaped by your desires or the desires of God? Explain.

3. How can you let God's desires for your life become your own desires?

Day four: Colossians 3:8-9

1. What word or phrase jumps out to you? Why?

2. Even though we know what's right, like not lying or losing our temper, why do you think we so easily fall into doing those things?

3. Take some time today and think about the concept of throwing away your old "clothes" and putting on the new "clothes" of your faith that God has given you. What does that look like in your life?

Day five: Colossians 3:10-12

1. What word or phrase jumps out to you? Why?

2. Is your life defined by Jesus or by your own rules?

3. What are some new "articles of clothing" in your life in God that you want to put on?

Day six: Colossians 3:13-15

1. What word or phrase jumps out to you? Why?

2. Paul says to be full of compassion, kindness, humility, and gentleness and to be quick to forgive. Why is this hard to do?

3. Take some time today and think about how God's forgiveness has changed your life. How should this affect the way you forgive others? (See Ephesians 4:32.)

Day seven: Colossians 3:1-15

Read through the entire passage. Write down the one verse that impacted you the most this week. Commit the passage to memory.

 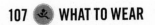

SESSION 19
Guidelines for Relationships: Colossians 3:16-25

LEADER'S INSIGHT

God designed us for relationships. Sometimes that's exciting; sometimes it's terrifying. Relationships can be messy and always demand growth. If we aren't growing individually, we aren't likely to be growing in relationships with other people. Conflicts come, and, apart from humility and growth, the relationship dies. Grow or die: This can be a harsh reality.

In Colossians 3:16-25, Paul gives instructions about relationships. He speaks to wives, husbands, children, parents, masters, and slaves. Paul gives specific instructions that, if followed, will lead to growth in relationships. If ignored, however, pain is inevitable. Paul urges husbands to "love your wives and do not be harsh with them" (verse 19). That was a radical teaching for that day because it gave women dignity.

Relationships without Jesus at the center are certain to struggle. Paul begins this passage by insisting that "the message of Christ dwell among you richly" (Colossians 3:16). Jesus makes all the difference in our relationships. As stated in Colossians 3:1-15, when we put on Jesus Christ, we will choose love over hate, forgiveness over resentment, kindness over meanness, peace over anger, and purity over lust.

This section of Scripture calls for our relationships to be whole and holy. Perhaps many of your students have never seen a godly, whole marriage. Maybe few have seen any solid models of marriage. Chances are, your group members are faced with conflict with their parents right now. Spend some quality time in this session examining relationships and coming up with some biblical guidelines to help make relationships God-honoring.

SHARE

- Which of your relationships are leading you toward life? Which might be leading you toward destruction?

- What relationships have most shaped your life thus far?

- If you wrote a list of guidelines for relationships, what would be your number one guideline?

OBSERVE

- Read Colossians 3:16-17. What do these two verses have to do with relationships?

- In verses 18-22 what five groups of people does Paul specifically address? Which groups describe you?

- In what things are children to obey their parents? In what things are slaves to obey their masters?

- According to verse 24, who are slaves actually serving?

THINK

- Look at verses 16-17. Why do you think Paul emphasizes to "let the word of Christ richly dwell among [us]" before we teach and admonish others?

- What do you think it means to submit to one another?

- What may happen to children who are treated harshly by their parents, particularly their fathers?

•Based on verses 22-25 is it okay to work lazily and apathetically if you don't like or disagree with the authority placed over you? Have you ever struggled with this? How?

APPLY

•Do you ever think about getting married? If yes, what qualities do you want in a marriage partner?

•Are you obedient to your parents? What are you responsible for that needs to change in your relationship with them?

•Ask God to help you consider what a godly marriage looks like in the future and ways to honor your parents creatively in the present. Share some of your ideas.

DO

Based on this passage, write out five guidelines for relationships. Brainstorm as a group other biblical guidelines for relationships. Work together to find the Scriptures that support these guidelines.

QUIET TIME REFLECTIONS

Day one: Colossians 3:16-17

1. What word or phrase jumps out to you? Why?

2. Look up the word *admonish*. What does it mean? How do you admonish others? Is this something you are good at?

3. Write a contemporary "psalm, hymn, or song from the Spirit" of gratitude. Share it with someone today.

Day two: Colossians 3:18

1. What word or phrase jumps out to you? Why?

2. Which couples you know have a healthy marriage? What makes you think that?

3. Spend some time praying for your future husband or wife. What qualities do you hope he or she has?

Day three: Colossians 3:19

1. What word or phrase jumps out to you? Why?

2. What are some of the effects of harsh parenting?

3. Whom do you know who's a great husband?

Day four: Colossians 3:20

1. What word or phrase jumps out to you? Why?

2. In what areas are children to obey their parents?

3. What does obeying our parents have to do with pleasing God? (See also Ephesians 6:1.)

Day five: Colossians 3:21

1. What word or phrase jumps out to you? Why?

2. What does it mean to embitter someone?

3. Think about the times you have felt discouraged by a parent. How did you handle the discouragement? How did that make you feel?

Day six: Colossians 3:22-25

1. What word or phrase jumps out to you? Why?

2. In what tasks do you easily work wholeheartedly? In what areas do you struggle to work wholeheartedly? What makes these situations different?

3. Think about the phrase "whatever you do, work at it...as working for the Lord." Write a definition of what this means for you, including how it should affect your life at home, at school, at church, while doing chores, at work, and in relationships.

Day seven: Colossians 3:16-25

Read through the entire passage. Write down the one verse that impacted you the most this week. Commit the passage to memory.

SESSION 20
Eyes Wide Open: Colossians 4:1-18

LEADER'S INSIGHT

The Christian journey isn't a call into the "holy huddle" in which we stay only with Christians—instead it's a community of people growing, learning, celebrating, and struggling together, then going out into the world and unleashing God's love. Paul closes his letter to the church in Colossae by urging them to pray and encourage one another and also to watch the way they live because their lives speak the loudest about their faith.

Paul begins chapter 4 by instructing the believers to be watchful and thankful. He asks them for prayer that God would guide and direct his ministry. Paul then challenges them to be wise in how they act toward outsiders, people who haven't put their faith in Jesus. He then goes on to send his greetings and encourage fellow "co-workers for the kingdom" (Colossians 4:11).

Fellowship is an overused word in the church today. It isn't "two fellows in a ship," nor does it mean "cookies and punch hour" between church services. The true meaning of the word *fellowship* is "commonness or communion." It means to share life together.

As followers of Jesus we should be entering into real and genuine relationships with one another. We should be wrestling in prayer (Colossians 4:2-5) and challenging each other with the hope of growing closer to the person of Jesus (4:7-14).

In Acts 2:42-47 we're told that because of the fellowship of the early church and their raw and authentic community, people were added to their number daily. How did these outsiders become insiders?

More importantly, why did they want to become insiders? They saw the community of Jesus followers interact. They saw wonders and miracles and deep sharing. All of the followers' needs were being met. If we're to impact the world, then we need to pour out love in our group, which then will spill over into a world watching with eyes wide open.

SHARE

•Who are your best friends? What's your favorite thing to do with them?

•Whom would you say you've influenced the most? How?

•When you think back on the times you've had with one of your best friends, what's your favorite story to tell?

OBSERVE

•According to Colossians 4:2-4, what does Paul tell us to devote ourselves to and why?

•Read verses 5-7. What's the result of acting wisely before outsiders?

•Why do you think Paul mentions Tychicus and Aristarchus and Justin and Epaphras in verses 7-12?

•According to verse 16, what does Paul want to be done with the letter after it has been read in Colossae? Why do you think he asks for this?

THINK

•Why does Paul ask for prayer from other believers?

•In verse 2 Paul says to be watchful and thankful. What are we to be watchful and thankful for?

•According to verse 5 what are some ways to act wisely toward outsiders?

•In verses 7-15 Paul passes on greetings to fellow believers. Why would he think this was an important thing to do?

APPLY

•How devoted to prayer are you?

•Who in your life has been the biggest source of encouragement? How has he done that?

•Whom could you encourage today and how could you do that?

DO

Have each person in the group think of three people who could use some encouragement and prayer. Have students take some time and write these people cards, telling them how the students feel about them and that they'll be praying for them. Pray as a group for each person and then send the cards (or a voice mail, email, or text message).

QUIET TIME REFLECTIONS

Day one: Colossians 4:1-4

1. What word or phrase jumps out to you? Why?

2. How important is prayer to you? When do you pray the most?

3. How often do you pray for others? How often do you ask them to pray for you?

Day two: Colossians 4:5-6

1. What word or phrase jumps out to you? Why?

2. Does your life display your faith in Jesus? How or how not?

3. What would it mean for your conversations to be full of grace and seasoned with salt?

Day three: Colossians 4:7-9

1. What word or phrase jumps out to you? Why?

2. How can you encourage someone's heart today?

3. Why is it important for you to share what God is doing in your life with your friends?

Day four: Colossians 4:10-11

1. What word or phrase jumps out to you? Why?

2. Do you sometimes feel as if you're the only one who lives a life for Jesus? How does that make you feel?

3. How are you a worker for the kingdom of God?

Day five: Colossians 4:12-15

1. What word or phrase jumps out to you? Why?

2. What does it mean to "stand firm in all the will of God"?

3. Based on verse 15, define what the church is called to be.

Day six: Colossians 4:16-18

1. What word or phrase jumps out to you? Why?

2. Why would Paul want this letter to be read in another church?

3. Think about Paul being in chains—why would he find this important?

Day seven: Colossians 4:1-18

Read through the entire passage. Write down the one verse that impacted you the most this week. Commit the passage to memory.

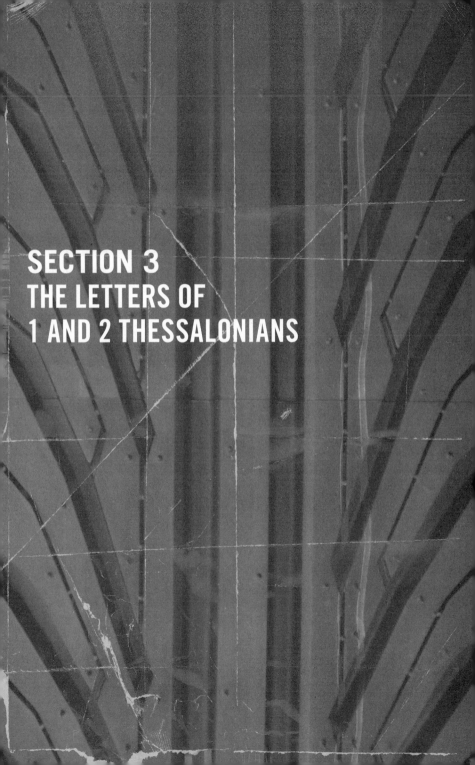

SECTION 3
THE LETTERS OF
1 AND 2 THESSALONIANS

HANDY TIPS AND INSIGHTS FOR 1 & 2 THESSALONIANS

WHO? These two letters to the Thessalonians (pronounced *thess-uh-lo-nee-unz* with a strong emphasis on *lo*) were written by Paul, who penned Philippians, Colossians, and other letters.

WHERE? Thessalonica was about 100 miles from Philippi. Thessalonica was one of the most significant military and commercial ports in the world at the time of Paul's letter. This thriving city was strategically centered on the Via Egnatia (Egnatian Way), a major travel route in the Roman Empire. The city had both great wealth and poverty. The city of Thessalonica is known today as Salonika, one of the largest cities in Greece.

WHEN? When Paul crossed into Macedonia around AD 50, Christianity was spreading into Greece, Italy, Spain, and Rome. When Paul left Philippi, he went to Thessalonica (along the Via Egnatia, the Roman military road across northern Greece). Paul's visit to start the church in Thessalonica is recorded in Acts 17. Paul wrote 1 Thessalonians from Corinth around AD 50-51 during his second missionary journey.

WHAT? Paul wrote this first letter to encourage the Christians. As it was a young "Jesus movement," Paul needed to address some problems: Sexual issues, moral issues, work issues, and theology issues. Aren't you glad we don't face these issues today?

These five chapters cover in essence what the church needed to know and learn to face:

> 1 Thessalonians 1—impact
>
> 1 Thessalonians 2—opposition

1 Thessalonians 3—faithfulness

1 Thessalonians 4—purity

1 Thessalonians 5—alert

The second letter to the Thessalonians contains a similar emphasis as the first letter. Written less than a year after 1 Thessalonians, this letter was also written from Corinth. It covers these three topics:

2 Thessalonians 1—Jesus is coming back

2 Thessalonians 2—Man of sin

2 Thessalonians 3—Life above mediocrity

SESSION 21
You Are the Message! 1 Thessalonians 1:1-10

LEADER'S INSIGHT

Have you ever had to say goodbye to someone, knowing you probably would never see them again? That's what was happening in this first letter to the Thessalonians. The apostle Paul started the church, but because of opposition, he sent his companion and friend Timothy to visit them.

Some have viewed Paul as a man of great faith and poor relational skills. 2 Corinthians 10:10 states, "For some say, 'His letters are weighty and forceful, but in person he is unimpressive and his speaking amounts to nothing.'" His speaking amounts to nothing?

Whatever could be said about Paul, whether personally unimpressive or a less than captivating speaker, he writes with words of affirmation and affection: "We always thank God for all of you and continually mention you in our prayers" (1 Thessalonians 1:2).

In 1 Corinthians Paul speaks of three great virtues of marriage: Faith, hope, and love. Paul mentions the same in this letter to encourage the believers to stand strong in their faith, hope, and love. As we share our faith, hope, and love, people are changed. We influence others by how we live. Paul explains in this chapter that we not only tell the message, but we also ARE the message.

Someone has said, "We might be the only Bible people ever read." Our students will be reminded that our lives really are under a microscope—others are watching how we live. And the question is, will people see something in our lives that would make them want to start a relationship with God?

SHARE

- What's your favorite way to connect with people: Phone, text message, email, or a personal visit?

- What are some of your favorite things to do with a friend?

- In what areas do you seem to need the most encouragement?

OBSERVE

- What's Paul bragging about in 1 Thessalonians 1:1-3?

- Read verses 4-6. What do you learn about the gospel of Jesus?

- According to verses 7-8, what's Paul's message to the Thessalonians?

- Look at verses 9-10. Based on this passage, what kind of change has occurred?

THINK

- Why do you suppose Paul seems always to start his letters off by remembering and thanking the church (see verses 1-3)?

- What do you think it means to be an "imitator of us and of the Lord" (verse 6)?

- Some say they want to imitate Jesus—but why? It seems like a hard way to live. What do you think?

- Paul mentions that some have turned from idols. What's an idol today? Which idol have you turned from or are you working on turning from?

APPLY

- Who has been one of the greatest influences on your life spiritually?

- If someone at your school was interviewed about you, what would he say about your faith and the way you live?

- Who's someone you might want to imitate to improve some area of your walk with God?

DO

Have each student create a list of first names of people who've made a major impact on him. Ask those who'd like to share some of the names they've listed and why. Then take a few minutes to go around the room and pray a prayer of thanks for these people.

QUIET TIME REFLECTIONS

Day one: 1 Thessalonians 1-2

1. What word or phrase jumps out to you? Why?

2. Why does Paul place prayer and thanksgiving together?

3. Think about how you can move from just making requests of God in your prayers to thanking him. What are some things you can thank God for?

Day two: 1 Thessalonians 1:3-4

1. What word or phrase jumps out to you? Why?

2. What qualities does Paul mention here?

3. Think about the word *endurance*. What does it mean, and how can you go after it (how can you gain endurance)?

Day three: 1 Thessalonians 1:5-6

1. What word or phrase jumps out to you? Why?

2. Why is God's power important for the Christian?

3. Think about some of the abuses of power in the world today. As Christians, how can we stay away from them?

Day four: 1 Thessalonians 1:7

1. What word or phrase jumps out to you? Why?

2. What does it mean to model the faith?

3. Think about some of the people who haven't done a good job of modeling their faith. How has that impacted you?

1. What word or phrase jumps out to you? Why?

2. Paul mentions that God's message "rang out" from them. What kind of messages ring from you? What would others say you talk about most often?

3. Think about one person you know whose faith has been obvious to many. How has that person's faith made a difference to you and others?

1. What word or phrase jumps out to you? Why?

2. What's an idol? What idols do you struggle with?

3. What are two ways to help people make changes in their lives?

Read through the entire passage. Write down the one verse that impacted you the most this week. Commit the passage to memory.

SESSION 22
Can God Trust Us? 1 Thessalonians 2:1-20

LEADER'S INSIGHT

Leadership. What comes to your mind when you think of this word? Who comes to your mind when you think of a leader? What kind of leader are you? What's your leadership style? Are you caring? Aggressive? Opinionated? Assertive or laid-back? Introverted or extroverted?

The apostle Paul was a leader, and he and Silas and Timothy, two other leaders, loved the church at Thessalonica. Paul reminds the church that he, Silas, and Timothy not only came and preached the word of God, but also truly lived out the gospel they were teaching. They weren't a burden to those they stayed with. They weren't greedy or impatient. Rather Paul and his friends were gentle, righteous, and blameless among the growing church in Thessalonica.

There are many books today about leadership. But this chapter helps us look at some of the characteristics of a biblical leader. Paul mentions that a great leader isn't deceptive or a people pleaser (1 Thessalonians 2:4); doesn't abuse power (verse 6); is a God pleaser (verse 4), gentle (verse 7), loving (verse 8), encouraging, comforting, and hardworking (verse 9); and urges others to live fully for Jesus (verse 12).

Paul commends his brothers and sisters in Jesus for showing leadership as they take the gospel to others and really try to live it out. The apostle reminds them that not everyone believes, and a great leader knows how to be affirming, authentic, and sensitive toward people's needs, especially those outside the faith of Christianity. Paul ends his thought by again telling his church how much he desires to be with them and how proud he is of them.

SHARE

•Did anyone share the truth about Jesus with you? How did he do it? Did you believe him? Why or why not?

•Have you ever tried sharing what God has done in your life? What was it like? How did you do it?

•Do you think there are good and bad ways of sharing biblical truth with people? What would be a good way?

OBSERVE

•Read verses 1-2. What was Paul trying to share with the Thessalonians?

•In verses 3-12, Paul makes a list of the ways he and friends acted while sharing the gospel. What are some of the things they did and didn't do?

•In verses 13-16, how do we see the church respond to Paul's teachings?

•In verses 17-20, what are some of the things that Paul tells the church? Do these sound positive or negative?

THINK

•Why do you think Paul is so passionate about sharing Jesus?

•Why do you think the Thessalonians responded so favorably to Paul and his teaching?

•How do you think Paul has earned the right to preach to the Thessalonians? How do you think the church responded to Paul correcting them?

•What do you think it means when Paul says the Thessalonians are his joy and glory?

APPLY

•Paul lists some specific ways in which he, Timothy, and Silas lived their faith. Which ones seem easy? Which ones would take more practice?

•Paul ends chapter 2 by speaking about how much he desires to be with the Thessalonians. Do you desire to be with people who don't yet know Jesus Christ or have just begun to walk with him?

•How can you be an imitator of God each day?

DO

Hand out paper to everyone and have each person make a list of friends and family she wants to see come closer to God. Then tell students to work back through 1 Thessalonians 2 and match up how Paul treated others when he was sharing God with them and how the students have treated the people on their lists. Then ask, **Can God trust you with the task of bearing his name to others who haven't heard? Does your lifestyle model and reflect Jesus?**

QUIET TIME REFLECTIONS

Day one: 1 Thessalonians 2:1-2

1. What word or phrase jumps out to you? Why?

2. What had Paul shared with the Thessalonians? Does it sound like it was easy to do?

3. Think about who introduced you to Jesus. How did he communicate the message? What did he say?

Day two: 1 Thessalonians 2:3-4

1. What word or phrase jumps out to you? Why?

2. Who is Paul trying to please? Why do you think he talks about motives?

3. Think about people you know who really love God. What makes them different? How do they act around those who don't believe?

Day three: 1 Thessalonians 2:5-8

1. What word or phrase jumps out to you? Why?

2. Make a list of the ways Paul influenced the Thessalonians. What do you think Paul means when he says, "We loved you so much, we were delighted to share with you not only the gospel of God but our lives as well"?

3. Think about your faith in Jesus. How do you model this to other people? How can you share your life and faith at the same time?

Day four: 1 Thessalonians 2:9-12

1. What word or phrase jumps out to you? Why?

2. What do you think Paul means by not being a burden?

3. Spend some time today thinking about your life. Are you involved in some kind of ministry to people? Why or why not?

Day five: 1 Thessalonians 2:13-16

1. What word or phrase jumps out to you? Why?

2. Do you think the way Paul presented the truth of Christ's message might have influenced the Thessalonians' response? Why or why not?

3. Spend some time today thinking about those you go to school with and work with. How might you share your faith in a way they can relate to?

Day six: 1 Thessalonians 2:17-20

1. What word or phrase jumps out to you? Why?

2. Does it sound as if Paul loved those he taught and served? What role does love play in serving and sharing our faith with others?

3. Paul considered sharing the gospel on a verbal level only part of the mission Jesus calls us to. What words and actions from your life reflect Jesus?

Day seven: 1 Thessalonians 2:1-20

Read through the entire passage. Write down the one verse that impacted you the most this week. Commit the passage to memory.

SESSION 23
Surprised by Trouble: 1 Thessalonians 3:1-13

LEADER'S INSIGHT

Trials. Trouble. Tribulation. Suffering. Paul continues his first letter to the Thessalonians with a detailed explanation of his concern for the believers, which prompted his sending Timothy to encourage them. Paul realized suffering and trouble often have a way of exposing areas of needed growth. His anxiety turned to joy after hearing Timothy's good news of their faith and love.

Paul's love for these believers is shown even more clearly by the intensity of his prayers on their behalf. His ultimate goal for this church was to see them walking as closely to Jesus as possible.

Life can be hard. Suffering will happen (Philippians 1:29 and 2 Corinthians 1:3-4). Jesus says today has enough trouble and not to worry about tomorrow (John 16:33 and Matthew 6:33-34). Where is God when life is rough?

We often don't know what to do with our pain. We desire life to be simple and pain-free. Students have their own sets of struggles: School, parent issues, fear of failure, fear of the future, academics, relationships, and how to have faith in a culture that seems rarely to think about God. When life throws tests at us, should we be surprised (1 Peter 4:12)? This section will explore how we should handle pain.

SHARE

- When you experience any trouble or pain, how do you usually react?

- Why do you think suffering is a part of being a Christian?

- Whom do you turn to when you're surprised by some difficulty?

OBSERVE

- Read 1 Thessalonians 3:1-5. How would you describe Paul's circumstances and concern for the Thessalonians? What actions did he take to relieve his concern?

- Based on verses 6-10, what details about the Thessalonians do we learn from Timothy's report to Paul?

- In verses 11-12, what prayer requests does Paul make?

- In verse 13, what qualities does Paul want to see in the lives of the believers when Jesus returns?

THINK

- What does Paul share about his purposes in sending Timothy in verses 2-5? What connection is there between Paul's suffering and his concern about their well-being?

- How does Paul respond to Timothy's report about the Thessalonians?

- Why do you think Christians need encouragement?

APPLY

•Who are the Timothys in your life? How do you respond to their help when they supply what's lacking in your faith?

•We know from this chapter that Paul prayed for believers and acted in love on their behalf. What does this teach us about our role in loving other believers and our friends?

•Paul ends this chapter by expressing his ultimate goal—that God would prepare the believers for meeting Jesus when he comes again. Why is this also important for your life? How can you grow in holiness even when you're surprised by trouble? How does the reality of Jesus' return further motivate us to walk in holiness?

DO

Pull out some Bible concordances and look to see how many Bible verses you can find related to Jesus' future return to earth. Write out the verses on a big sheet of paper and have the group look up and study the verses. Then ask the group, **What's one new thing you learned about Jesus' coming back? What's one thing you must change to get ready for Jesus' return?**

QUIET TIME REFLECTIONS

Day one: 1 Thessalonians 3:1-3

1. What word or phrase jumps out to you? Why?

2. What's Paul concern in this part of the letter? What clues in Paul's words indicate that the Thessalonians needed a little help? How does this relate to your faith life?

3. Spend some time today thinking about how trials can unsettle our faith. Whom do you turn to when you're surprised by troubles?

Day two: 1 Thessalonians 3:4-6

1. What word or phrase jumps out to you? Why?

2. How would you describe Paul's motive for sending Timothy to the Thessalonians? What report did Timothy bring to him?

3. Who are people who hold you in great affection, like Paul held the Thessalonians? Consider writing a note of thanks to one of these special people who loves you and is concerned for your well-being.

Day three: 1 Thessalonians 3:7-8

1. What word or phrase jumps out to you? Why?

2. How do you think the believers might have felt, knowing Paul's love and concern for them, even though his own circumstances were filled with difficulty? How could having these types of friends in your life encourage you to keep following Jesus during tough times?

3. What distress or trouble are you currently going through? Ask God to send faithful leaders and friends like Paul and Timothy to you, so your faith may remain strong during tough times.

Day four: 1 Thessalonians 3:9-10

1. What word or phrase jumps out to you? Why?

2. How would you describe the mood of Paul's prayer? What was his motive for wanting to go see the Thessalonians? How does this relate to your life?

3. Ask God to help you identify the area you most need to have a spiritual tune-up. What is it? Ask a friend to help you be accountable to make a change in this area of growth.

Day five: 1 Thessalonians 2:11-12

1. What word or phrase jumps out to you? Why?

2. Why is it essential for us to bring our needs to God in prayer? How can prayer help us live a life increasing and overflowing in love for others and for God?

3. Spend some time in prayer, especially asking God to increase your love for others and, most importantly, for God. If you feel your capacity to love is shallow, ask God to increase it and allow it to overflow.

Day six: 1 Thessalonians 3:13

1. What word or phrase jumps out to you? Why?

2. What does Paul ask for? How does Paul want to see the believers prepared to meet Jesus when he returns? How does this relate to your preparation to meet Jesus someday?

3. Who are you in Jesus? How are you getting ready to meet him on a daily basis? Is your life filled with holiness? Ask God to fill you with a fresh, daily purity from the Holy Spirit right now.

Day seven: 1 Thessalonians 3:1-13

Read through the entire passage. Write down the one verse that impacted you the most this week. Commit the passage to memory.

SESSION 24
Life Together: 1 Thessalonians 4:1-18

LEADER'S INSIGHT

College life. Dorm living. The two are not always fun. Having a roommate or living with someone at summer camp may be one of the best ways to get to know yourself and others better. It reveals what's truly in your heart. Living in a community with other people brings out your best and worst qualities.

Paul seems to key in on both of these areas in this passage. Paul takes the time to remind the Christians in Thessalonica, as well as us, that God has certain criteria for living life together. He instructs us to control our bodies (1 Thessalonians 4:4), show concern for one another (verse 6), and love each other like God loves us (verse 9). When we live rightly, we please God. We're called to live wholly and in sexual purity (verse 3).

As disciples living in community with one another from neighborhoods to shopping centers, Paul encourages us constantly to keep one thought in mind. In 1 Thessalonians 4:9-12, the apostle Paul tells us how to live our faith to those he refers to as outsiders. These outsiders not only are outside the faith of Christ, but also probably don't understand it. We're to live in a way that makes outsiders eventually want to be insiders.

Paul reminds us in 1 Thessalonians 4:13-18 that when Jesus Christ returns, he will unite those who've passed away with those who are alive: "For the Lord himself will come down from heaven, with a loud command" (verse 16). With this in mind, Paul says, we should take great concern with how we live our lives. After all, living as Christians was never meant to be done alone.

SHARE

- Share a time when you've spent enormous numbers of days and hours with a particular group of people, for example, on a sleepover, mission trip, your family vacation, etc.

- What's the hardest part about living in the same space with other people? What's the best part about it?

- In what ways do you think you're easy to live with? In what ways might you be difficult to live with?

OBSERVE

- From 1 Thessalonians 4:2, by what authority does Paul speak?

- What's Paul urging for these Christians in verses 3-8?

- What does Paul say will result from living a quiet and hardworking life?

- What's happening in verses 13-18?

THINK

- What does the word *sanctified* mean? How does following the instructions of God lead to sanctification?

- In verse 13, Paul speaks of some who grieve over death. What causes their grief? What hope are we given in the midst of grief?

- Why does Paul instruct the Thessalonians to "encourage one another with these words" (verse 18)?

APPLY

- What's one way you've pleased God? How did you feel after you did it?

- Paul talks about our living a pure life in verse 7. How do we become pure before God?

- Have you ever shared the hope of Jesus' return with someone you know? How did they respond?

- What encouragement did you get from reading this passage of Scripture?

DO

Hand out a piece of paper and pen or pencil to each student. Then take the group through this exercise, saying something like, **Write down five nonphysical qualities about yourself that you'd like to change. Then write down five qualities God has that you'd like to have. Finally, write down how obtaining the five new qualities and getting rid of the five old qualities would impact the relationships you have with other people.**

QUIET TIME REFLECTIONS

Day one: 1 Thessalonians 4:1-2

1. What word or phrase jumps out to you? Why?

2. How did you live today to please God? How could you have lived better?

3. Think about instructions the Bible gives us on how to live. What's the most difficult for you at this moment?

Day two: 1 Thessalonians 4:3-5

1. What word or phrase jumps out to you? Why?

2. What does "sanctified" mean?

3. How can you use your body to honor God?

Day three: 1 Thessalonians 4:6-8

1. What word or phrase jumps out to you? Why?

2. How have you wronged someone this week? How could you have changed the outcome? What can you do to bring forgiveness?

3. Think about why God wants us to live holy lives. How does that make you into what God intends for you to be?

Day four: 1 Thessalonians 4:9-12

1. What word or phrase jumps out to you? Why?

2. What image comes to mind when you think of the word *love*? What do you think it means that "God is love"?

3. What does gaining others' respect do for your message of Jesus? Is gaining respect difficult or easy?

Day five: 1 Thessalonians 4:13-14

1. What word or phrase jumps out to you? Why?

2. Have you had a loved one pass away in your lifetime? What has helped you cope with the loss?

3. What do Jesus' death and resurrection have to do with us and the mission of the church?

Day six: 1 Thessalonians 4:15-18

1. What word or phrase jumps out to you? Why?

2. Do you believe Jesus will come back? Why or why not? How often do you think about Jesus returning? How can this be a source of joy?

3. What do you think about heaven and the afterlife? Do you think about it at all? Too little? Too much? Is thinking about heaven a way to escape life now for you, or is it a great relief and excitement?

Day seven: 1 Thessalonians 4:1-18

Read through the entire passage. Write down the one verse that impacted you the most this week. Commit the passage to memory.

[From *Studies on the Go: The Letters of Philippians, Colossians, and 1 and 2 Thessalonians* by Dr. David Olshine. Permission to reproduce this page granted only for use in buyer's youth group. Copyright ©2009 by Youth Specialties.]

 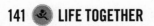

SESSION 25
No Sleepwalking: 1 Thessalonians 5:1-11

LEADER'S INSIGHT

Many people are afraid of closed-in spaces, snakes, terrorism, singleness, marriage, and the future. Many are more afraid of public speaking than dying!

Most of us don't like the uncertainty of what's to come, but we can be sure of one thing. The Bible declares a reality: Jesus Christ will return. The promise of his coming also creates more questions than answers. When will Jesus come? Will it be in my lifetime? What's the "day of the Lord"? What will it be like? We question when it will be, what will take place, who it will affect.

Paul takes time in his letter to the Thessalonians to clear up any misunderstanding about the future of Jesus' return and to encourage and instruct us on holy living.

In this session your students will determine what it means to live this life fully awake, eagerly anticipating the return of Jesus. We'll talk about how to deal with the things we know are certain and how to deal with uncertainty. It's time to set our alarm clocks and open our eyes to the life God has called us to live. We're alive in Jesus Christ: "So then, let us not be like others, who are asleep, but let us be awake and sober" (1 Thessalonians 5:6). This life isn't made for sleepwalking. It's time to wake up!

SHARE

- Are you someone who likes to know what's going to happen, or do you love being spontaneous?

- Are you a morning person or a night person? What morning routines do you have?

- What makes you most anxious in life?

OBSERVE

- Read 1 Thessalonians 5:1-3. What are some words that come to mind to describe the return of Jesus? What does Paul have to say about when it will be?

- According to verses 4-8, what's our responsibility as Christians?

- Based on verses 9-10, what's the result of Jesus' death?

- What kinds of words are we supposed to speak to each other? In verse 11, whom does Paul say to include?

THINK

- Verse 2 refers to a "thief in the night." Why do you think Paul describes Jesus' return like this?

- What do you think being the "children of light" means?

- Look at verses 7-9. How do people of the night act? What makes Christians different?

- Verse 11 tells us to encourage each other. What are some ways to do this?

APPLY

- How have you been sleepwalking though life?

- What are some ways you could wake yourself up?

- Can you think of some friends who need a wake-up call? What are some ways you could encourage them?

- What are some ways our culture is sleepwalking?

DO

Walk your group outside. Put the group into pairs and give each pair a blindfold. Then explain the instructions: One person will lead; the other will be blindfolded. Pair mates can't talk to each other. No one can speak. The leader should take the follower by the arm and lead her. The follower has to learn to trust the leader. Do this for several minutes. Then reverse roles and have the other person do the same with the blindfold. Then debrief the experience as a group.

QUIET TIME REFLECTIONS

Day one: 1 Thessalonians 5:1-2

1. What word or phrase jumps out to you? Why?

2. Why do you think people disagree so much about the day of Jesus' return?

3. Think about what that day will be like. Do you think you're ready for it? Why or why not?

Day two: 1 Thessalonians 5:3-4

1. What word or phrase jumps out to you? Why?

2. Think about the pain Paul talks about. Why would that day be painful?

3. Think about the differences between darkness and light. How are we (Christians) different from others?

Day three: 1 Thessalonians 5:5

1. What word or phrase jumps out to you? Why?

2. Whom do we belong to? What's special about that?

3. We don't belong to the darkness, but we are drawn to it. What draws you into the darkness?

Day four: 1 Thessalonians 5:6-7

1. What word or phrase jumps out to you? Why?

2. What do you think it means to be alert and ready on a daily basis?

3. Define self-control. How does God help us to gain greater self-control? How can you let God be more in control?

Day five: 1 Thessalonians 5:8-9

1. What word or phrase jumps out to you? Why?

2. Paul says we aren't to receive wrath, but salvation. Why do we still struggle?

3. Think about how to arm yourself with faith, love, and hope. What does that look like or how does that work in your life?

Day six: 1 Thessalonians 5:10-11

1. What word or phrase jumps out to you? Why?

2. How has Jesus' death changed you?

3. Think about why Jesus died for everyone. Does that mean everyone is going to heaven? Does that make you think differently about how you are to love others?

Day seven: 1 Thessalonians 5:1-11

Read through the entire passage. Write down the one verse that impacted you the most this week. Commit the passage to memory.

SESSION 26
What Is God's Will? 1 Thessalonians 5:12-28

LEADER'S INSIGHT

I think most youth workers and church leaders would agree the number one question asked by students is, "How can I know the will of God?" When students ask this question, what they really seem to be asking is, "How do I know who I should marry? What college should I attend? Will I end up like my youth pastor who is balding?"

This section from 1 Thessalonians describes the practical nuts and bolts of what the will of God is really about: Living in the moment. This passage will help us explore a few "will of God" concepts, such as respecting leaders, living in peace, warning the idle, encouraging the timid, and being patient.

Listen to this passage: "Rejoice always, pray continually, give thanks in all circumstances; for this is God's will for you in Christ Jesus" (1 Thessalonians 5:16-18). I know we all have bad days, but this passage seems to suggest that when we're whiny, ungrateful, unthankful, and complaining, we're outside of God's will.

In this session your students will discover the will of God isn't about pie-in-the-sky theology or escapism into the next life, but living in the here and now. The will of God, according to this text, isn't about which college to choose or what city to live in, although those are important. The will of God is about how we live connected to God and each other—today. "Make sure that nobody pays back wrong for wrong, but always strive to do what is good for each other and for everyone else" (1 Thessalonians 5:15). The will of God is about our attitudes in life and how we respond to life's hardships.

SHARE

- If you could find out one thing about the future, what would it be?

- Why is it hard for us to decide what to do with our lives?

- What do you think about people who seem to know what they should do when they grow up when they're just 10 or 11 years old?

OBSERVE

- According to 1 Thessalonians 5:12-14, what should be our attitude toward leaders and toward those who are constantly struggling?

- Based on verses 15-18, what's the will of God, according to Paul?

- Look at verses 19-23. Describe God's plan for our lives.

- What's Paul saying in verses 24-28 about relationships?

THINK

- What do you think it means to hold leaders in the highest regard?

- Who does Paul focus on in verses 14-15? Why do you think he does this?

- Why do you think we aren't to pay back wrong with wrong (verse 15)?

- What does it mean that we should "rejoice always, pray continually and give thanks in all circumstances" (verses 16-18)? Is that really possible?

APPLY

- Who do you relate to more, the hardworking leader or the lazy and disruptive person? Why?

- What are some ways to encourage the disheartened, help the weak, and be patient with everyone?

- If we are to give thanks for everything, how can we be thankful in the face of difficult stuff like cancer, hurricanes, death, AIDS, and disabilities?

- If God's will is to rejoice, pray continually, and give thanks in all circumstances, does this mean we're often outside of the will of God?

DO

Bring in a bunch of magazines (*People, Seventeen, Rolling Stone,* etc.), scissors, and glue. Have your students cut out pictures to put together a collage on posterboard titled "In the will of God" and another one titled "Outside of the will of God." Have your students look past styles and trends and try to get to the heart of what they sense the pictures are revealing.

QUIET TIME REFLECTIONS

Day one: 1 Thessalonians 5:12-13

1. What word or phrase jumps out to you? Why?

2. Why do you think Paul wants us to acknowledge our spiritual leaders?

3. How can you affirm and encourage your leaders today?

Day two: 1 Thessalonians 5:14-15

1. What word or phrase jumps out to you? Why?

2. Can you think of someone at church, youth group, or school who fits the description of verse 14?

3. How might you encourage this person (from question 2)?

Day three: 1 Thessalonians 5:16-18

1. What word or phrase jumps out to you? Why?

2. How does Paul describe the will of God?

3. What are some ways to put into practice the will of God based on verses 16-18?

Day four: 1 Thessalonians 5:19-22

1. What word or phrase jumps out to you? Why?

2. What are some ways, according to verses 19-22, to keep the Spirit's fire alive?

3. List some of the ways we can "hold on to what is good" and "reject what is harmful."

Day five: 1 Thessalonians 5:23-24

1. What word or phrase jumps out to you? Why?

2. What was God's purpose in calling us to be faithful?

3. In what ways might you be more "blameless"?

Day six: 1 Thessalonians 5:25-28

1. What word or phrase jumps out to you? Why?

2. According to this verse, people used to greet each other with a holy kiss. Why don't we still do this ancient custom? What would happen if we did? What do we do instead? Do you think it's as meaningful?

3. Think about someone who needs your prayers. Who is it and why? Lift him up to God in prayer today.

Day seven: 1 Thessalonians 5:12-28

Read through the entire passage. Write down the one verse that impacted you the most this week. Commit the passage to memory.

SESSION 27
Getting Fit: 2 Thessalonians 1:1-12

LEADER'S INSIGHT

Exercise: Do you love it or hate it? Our muscles are really good at letting us know when we've done something to make them stronger. They hurt—I mean really hurt—but because of the struggle and tension, the muscles grow stronger and more useful. Pain and hardship have this same strange way of refining and making us stronger.

Why doesn't God change my situation? Paul begins his second letter to the Thessalonians by encouraging the believers for their faith and perseverance in the midst of persecution. Faith and perseverance are muscles. If we use them, we grow. If not, our "muscles" atrophy. The muscles wear thin and become useless flab.

God doesn't try to change our circumstances; he tries to change us! The church in Thessalonica was one Paul says he boasted about because of their strength and what was being accomplished because of their resolve (2 Thessalonians 1:4). Paul reassures the believers their struggles aren't in vain and someday God's judgment will be delivered. He concludes the passage (verses 1-12) by giving the result of perseverance: God is glorified, and we're made more like Jesus.

Throughout the church's history nothing has caused it to grow like persecution. When believers persevere during difficult times, God is glorified and the kingdom of God is advanced. C.S. Lewis wrote, "God whispers in our pleasures, speaks in our conscience, but shouts in our pains: it is His megaphone to rouse a deaf world" (*The Problem of Pain*, New York: MacMillan, 1970, p. 26).

Pain and suffering get our attention and make us get in touch with our questions and need for God. In suffering many people ultimately find themselves in the place we belong—at the feet of our Savior. Jesus promised persecution on account of him (Mark 13). It will come. The question is: How will we respond when it comes? How fit are you?

SHARE

•When was the last time your body was sore? Why was it sore?

•Who's your favorite athlete? Why?

•How do you usually respond to opposition in your life?

OBSERVE

•Why does Paul thank God for the Thessalonians?

•Read 2 Thessalonians 1:4. What does Paul boast about?

•According to verse 5, why were the believers suffering?

•Why does Paul pray for the believers in verse 11?

THINK

•What is perseverance (verse 4)?

•From verse 5, what's the evidence for God's judgment?

•According to verse 6, why is God just?

•Read verses 11 and 12. What's the purpose of believers' suffering, according to these verses?

APPLY

- Are you currently suffering any sort of persecution for your faith? If so, how?

- How do you respond to God during difficult times?

- Do you welcome challenges or avoid them?

- How does perseverance during hard times glorify God?

DO

Have everyone in the group write down their three biggest fears in life and then think of ways God answers those fears. Share with the group.

QUIET TIME REFLECTIONS

Day one: 2 Thessalonians 1:1-3

1. What word or phrase jumps out to you? Why?

2. Why would Paul thank God for the love the believers have for each other?

3. How do you show love to other believers?

Day two: 2 Thessalonians 1:4

1. What word or phrase jumps out to you? Why?

2. How would you define perseverance?

3. What do you think perseverance takes?

Day three: 2 Thessalonians 1:5-7

1. What word or phrase jumps out to you? Why?

2. Do you believe God is just? Why or why not?

3. How does the idea of Jesus' return make you feel?

Day four: 2 Thessalonians 1:8-10

1. What word or phrase jumps out to you? Why?

2. Do you think it's fair that those who don't believe will be punished? Why or why not?

3. Why does God allow bad things to happen in this world? How do you respond when asked about this?

Day five: 2 Thessalonians 1:11

1. What word or phrase jumps out to you? Why?

2. What does it mean to be worthy of God's calling?

3. Do you feel worthy of God's calling? Why or why not?

Day six: 2 Thessalonians 1:12

1. What word or phrase jumps out to you? Why?

2. How do we glorify the name of Jesus through our lives?

3. Pray that the name of Jesus will be glorified in you and you in him.

Day seven: 2 Thessalonians 1:1-12

Read through the entire passage. Write down the one verse that impacted you the most this week. Commit the passage to memory.

SESSION 28
Out of Control: 2 Thessalonians 2:1-10

LEADER'S INSIGHT

Disasters: An earthquake hit China, killing over 20,000 people. A tsunami hit Thailand, leaving hundreds dead and thousands homeless. We wonder, "Why, God?" Terrorists flew planes into buildings on September 11, 2001, and thousands died. A mother drowned her children in a lake. On May 8, 2008, a cyclone hit Myanmar (formerly known as Burma) and left thousands dead and over a million homeless.

What on earth is going on? We start asking questions. Is this the beginning of the end? Or is it the end? Why are so many things out of control? Why do we have cable networks dedicated to letting us know how bad things really are? Are these signs of the end? How do we face and welcome the unknown? What will the end be like? Will there be a future?

In 2 Thessalonians 2:1-10 Paul encourages the Thessalonians to gain control of their thoughts, beliefs, and questions. He seeks to calm their fears by reminding them of truth, then sharing with them clear warning signs of the end times. Then Paul brings some clarity about the return of Jesus and the "day of the Lord."

1 Thessalonians 5:2 mentions that Jesus will come like a "thief in the night." Paul also mentions in 2 Thessalonians 2:1-10 the coming of the "man of lawlessness." Who is this man? What will he be like?

This section explores how Paul lovingly and affectionately reached out to the church at Thessalonica, seeking to bring them to a place of trust in Jesus rather than fear of the unknown.

SHARE

- What events in recent history make you think the world is out of control?

- Has there ever been a time in your life when you felt out of control? Explain.

- What do you feel and think when people talk about the end of the world?

OBSERVE

- According to 2 Thessalonians 2:1-2, who is Paul addressing and what is his concern?

- What's Paul saying in verses 3-6?

- Whom do you think the lawless one is associated with, according to verses 7-10?

- According to verses 8-10, what happens to those who don't believe the truth?

THINK

- What will be one dominant trait of the man of lawlessness?

- What does verse 6 reveal to us about God's power over the end times?

- How will Jesus overthrow the lawless one?

- What things will the lawless one use to deceive people who are perishing?

APPLY

- Have you ever felt unsettled about the end times? What questions and fears do you have?

- What frightens you most about the man of lawlessness?

- In what area of your life are you most vulnerable to believing lies?

- What are some ways to choose loving the truth and not believing the lies?

DO

Create a list of recent events around the world that have caused the world to seem out of control. Discuss the effects of these circumstances. How did people react? How did they treat each other? What did they cling to for hope and understanding? Spend time together praying for these people and their circumstances.

QUIET TIME REFLECTIONS

Day one: 2 Thessalonians 2:1-2

1. What word or phrase jumps out to you? Why?

2. What do you think this passage is about?

3. How are Christians being deceived today?

Day two: 2 Thessalonians 2:3-4

1. What word or phrase jumps out to you? Why?

2. Do you think the man of lawlessness is a future evil person or more of a symbol of something? Explain.

3. What are some ways people follow lawlessness?

Day three: 2 Thessalonians 2:5-6

1. What word or phrase jumps out to you? Why?

2. According to Paul, when will the man of lawlessness be revealed?

3. How do you think this revelation will affect the rest of the world?

Day four: 2 Thessalonians 2:7-8

1. What word or phrase jumps out to you? Why?

2. When will the secret power of lawlessness begin its work?

3. How do you think Jesus will overthrow the lawless one?

Day five: 2 Thessalonians 2:9

1. What word or phrase jumps out to you? Why?

2. Whom does the lawless one work with?

3. What are some of the lies you believe about yourself?

Day six: 2 Thessalonians 2:10

1. What word or phrase jumps out to you? Why?

2. Why does God allow people to be deceived?

3. Why do some follow the truth and others follow wickedness?

Day seven: 2 Thessalonians 2:1-10

Read through the entire passage. Write down the one verse that impacted you the most this week. Commit the passage to memory.

SESSION 29
Heads Lifted High: 2 Thessalonians 2:11-17

LEADER'S INSIGHT

In this section Paul continues his writings to the church on the subject of "the man of lawlessness." The Thessalonians were struggling over the future and what was to come. In the previous passage (2 Thessalonians 2:1-10) Paul has reminded the Thessalonians many people will follow "the man of lawlessness" and be led to destruction because of their wicked ways. But from verse 11 to the end of the chapter, Paul praises the church for choosing to follow Jesus to salvation and freedom. Paul reminds the Thessalonians God will strengthen those who have faith in his son, who cling to God's teachings for the times ahead.

The lawless one, often referred to as the antichrist, will have great power. He is filled with Satan, according to verse 9, and will have counterfeit signs, miracles, and wonders. Paul tells the people of God to stand firm against evil.

Times must've seemed very difficult for the church of Thessalonica. Paul had encouraged the Roman church "that all things work together for good to those who love God, who have been called according to his purpose" (Romans 8:28, footnote translation). Paul also encourages the Thessalonian church as he gives instructions on ways to handle tough times and how to keep focused in the face of evil. How did they respond, and how should we respond?

SHARE

•Do you ever worry about what the future holds?

•Is the world getting better or worse? How?

•Do you think there's a real Devil or Satan? Why or why not? Is Satan at work in the world today? How?

OBSERVE

•Read 2 Thessalonians 2:11-12. What kind of delusion is being talked about here?

•From verses 13-15, has Paul talked about the subject of the future before to the Thessalonians?

•In verse 16, what's the message from Paul to the Christians?

•In verse 17, what do we learn about hope and God's grace?

THINK

•What does Paul say about the lawless one in verses 11-12?

•Whom does it sound like the lawless one serves?

•Based on what Paul says in this passage, how do you think the church should respond regarding the future? Should we be worried?

•Why do you think people worry about the future?

APPLY

- According to Paul, who do you think is really in control of the future?

- How do you respond to the future? Do you fear what might happen?

- We know from this chapter that God is in control and in the end he punishes the wicked, but how are we as believers supposed to act before that happens?

- Paul ends chapter 2 by praising the Thessalonians for their choice of salvation, but he also encourages them to stay firm. How can you stand firm? What can help you stand firm, according to verses 13-17?

DO

Challenge your students by saying something like, **This week, use Paul's encouragement to the Thessalonians in verses 11-17 to help strengthen you so you can stand firm. Spend 20 minutes each day this week reading the Bible and spending time with God. The future Paul talks about sounds very dark and difficult. But we're told by Paul that God's Word strengthens and encourages us.**

QUIET TIME REFLECTIONS

Day one: 1 Thessalonians 2:11-12

1. What word or phrase jumps out to you? Why?

2. What's Paul speaking about in this section? Does it seem like the Thessalonians were a little confused on this subject?

3. Spend some time today thinking about future events. Whom do we trust with the future?

Day two: 2 Thessalonians 2:13

1. What word or phrase jumps out to you? Why?

2. What do you learn about God's choosing and loving us?

3. Spend some time today thinking about God choosing us rather than our choosing God. How does this make you feel?

Day three: 2 Thessalonians 2:14

1. What word or phrase jumps out to you? Why?

2. What does it mean to share in the glory of Jesus?

3. Spend some time today thinking about your belief in Jesus. How often do you do things for God's glory?

Day four: 2 Thessalonians 2:15

1. What word or phrase jumps out to you? Why?

2. What does it mean to stand firm? Why do you think some remain strong and others don't?

3. Spend some time today thinking about your life. What do you fear? Has God chosen you to share his gospel? What does it take to stand firm?

Day five: 2 Thessalonians 2:16

1. What word or phrase jumps out to you? Why?

2. What does Paul say about the character and nature of God the Father toward us?

3. Spend some time today thinking about this passage. How does it help you? What does it mean to have eternal encouragement and good hope?

Day six: 2 Thessalonians 2:17

1. What word or phrase jumps out to you? Why?

2. What does Paul ask for? Do you think God gives that? Have you ever seen those gifts from God?

3. Reflect today on who you are in Jesus. How has God reshaped some of your goals and desires?

Day seven: 2 Thessalonians 2:11-17

Read through the entire passage. Write down the one verse that impacted you the most this week. Commit the passage to memory.

SESSION 30
Moonlighting: 2 Thessalonians 3:1-18

LEADER'S INSIGHT

It. What is "it"? Sometime around the month of November and the month of May, "it" happens. A peculiar phenomenon affects some students, despite their years of study. As if staying engaged in schoolwork isn't hard enough, these particular students begin to focus on the Christmas or summer break, allowing laziness to set in. "It" is idleness.

In 2 Thessalonians 3 Paul begins by urging the believers to pray for God's protection from evil deeds in evil days. Paul bases his trust and hope on God himself. With God's protection and aid comes a responsibility for us to exercise proper living. Many of the Thessalonian believers were focused on the second coming of Jesus, and they were beginning to believe false teachings on such topics and give in to lazy living. The end seemed near or perhaps had already come—so they took time off.

Paul warns not only the lazy, but also those who associate with the lazy. Paul uses himself as an example by saying he didn't expect others to take care of him. He worked day and night in order not to be a burden to anyone. "Don't permit them to freeload on the rest...in fact, we worked our fingers to the bone, up half the night moonlighting so you wouldn't be burdened with taking care of us" (2 Thessalonians 3:6-8 MSG). He's saying to the lazy: Rather than taking time off, in thinking of Jesus' return and the great needs of those around you, how can you afford to be idle?

Paul recommends living full of energy and awareness. Then others may be drawn to live the same way. To end this heartfelt letter, Paul reminds his readers that God is in their corner. Paul's closing remarks can be summed up this way: No moonlighting—this is no time to become lazy, so get back to your passion for God with hard work.

SHARE

•What activity enables you to relax the most and why?

•If asked, how do you think the following people would rate your laziness on a scale of 1 (not lazy at all) to 10 (lazy all the time)? Dad or Mom? Sibling? Your teachers? Your best friend?

•Who is the hardest-working person you know? What drives her to work so hard?

OBSERVE

•Read 2 Thessalonians 3:5. What two things does Paul pray God will direct the believers into?

•According to Paul's instructions, how should we respond to a believer who's idle and unresponsive to godly commands?

•Verses 14-15 give guidelines on how to keep others accountable. What instructions do you see?

THINK

•What do you think of the principle Paul presents in verse 10: "Anyone who is unwilling to work shall not eat"? Is this a rule you would like to see enforced? How? What about people who cannot work?

•Why is Paul so strongly against idleness and disruption? Why are these two attitudes so troublesome?

•From verse 15, what's the difference between treating someone as an enemy and treating someone as a fellow believer? Which is easier? Why?

•How can God give peace in all circumstances?

APPLY

•Where do you spend most of your time during the day? How is that time beneficial?

•Which of these activities is the easiest for you to be lazy about and why?

> A. schoolwork
>
> B. job
>
> C. chores
>
> D. time with God
>
> E. _____

•What's one area of your life that needs to become more energetic and productive this week?

DO

Each morning for the next week, spend time getting focused on the day and ways to be productive. Pray only the line from the Lord's Prayer that says, "Your kingdom come, your will be done, on earth as it is in heaven." After praying this line a few times, make a list on a sheet of paper you can fit into your pocket or purse of all the ways you can live today that might cause God's kingdom to be present in your life.

QUIET TIME REFLECTIONS

Day one: 2 Thessalonians 3:1-2

1. What word or phrase jumps out to you? Why?

2. How would you sum up the "message of the Lord" in a few sentences? How can you honor that message?

3. What do you need God to deliver you from today?

Day two: 2 Thessalonians 3:3-5

1. What word or phrase jumps out to you? Why?

2. In what ways have you seen God being faithful in your life? In others' lives?

3. How can you make perseverance a part of your life today?

Day three: 2 Thessalonians 3:6-7

1. What word or phrase jumps out to you? Why?

2. What areas of your life do you recognize as idle? What would energize them?

3. Think about what it means to be idle as a Christian. Why is it dangerous to be idle?

Day four: 2 Thessalonians 3:8-10

1. What word or phrase jumps out to you? Why?

2. Whom would you look to as a healthy example of a godly, productive worker?

3. After reading verse 10, according to your productiveness today, would your belly be full or would you be going hungry?

Day five: 2 Thessalonians 3:11-13

1. What word or phrase jumps out to you? Why?

2. How can idleness lead to disruption? Which is more harmful?

3. What are ways to "never tire of doing what is good"? What was something you did recently that you'd call "doing good"?

Day six: 2 Thessalonians 3:14-18

1. What word or phrase jumps out to you? Why?

2. How can you not regard people as enemies but "warn them as fellow believers"? What does this require of you?

3. Where do you need God's peace in your life today?

Day seven: 2 Thessalonians 3:1-18

Read through the entire passage. Write down the one verse that impacted you the most this week. Commit the passage to memory.

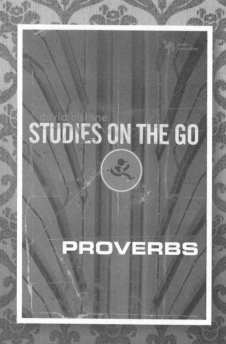

STUDIES ON THE GO

PROVERBS

Written with the busy youth worker in mind, books in the Studies on the Go series will provide Scriptural depth and substance to be tackled in a manageable time frame. The questions are real and get straight to the point. As students study Proverbs, they will learn that knowledge is not enough—they also need God's wisdom to handle daily challenges.

Studies on the Go: Proverbs

David Olshine
978-0-310-28548-9
Retail $8.99

Visit www.youthspecialties.com
or your local bookstore.

youth
specialties

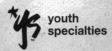

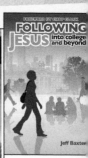